The contents of this book were originally found in the Gospel according to Matthew, Mark, Luke, and John, which were written under the influence of the Holy Spirit. For "All scripture is given by inspiration of God (who is Spirit), and is profitable for doctrine, for reproof, for correction, for instruction in righteousness that the man (all-inclusive [man and wo-man]) of God may be perfect, thoroughly furnished unto all good works. 2 Timothy 3:16-17

These are not new scriptures, nor a new doctrine. Furthermore, this book is not the Bible, nor a fifth gospel. Instead, it is a harmonized narrative that combines all four gospels into one continuous and chronological account such that it is easier to understand and use for study and easy referencing. Much care was taken to avoid adding any element that did not serve the specific purpose of harmonizing the four Gospel accounts into one seamless chronicle. That is not to say there is no bonus content, or notes, but they are infrequent.

I thank God for His nearness. Scripture teaches in Psalm 73:28 that "it is good to be near God." It is in drawing closer to Him, that I am still learning to love the LORD more daily (for He is good indeed), and to fear the LORD, for this is the beginning of wisdom. Since this book's sole purpose is to help readers better harmonize and understand the Gospel accounts as one seamless narrative from four perspectives instead of four different "stories," and because these accounts were not written (but merely sequenced and compiled) by me, I refuse to take credit as the "author." Instead, I humbly accept the role of compiler of this book. Neither will I dedicate this particular book to anyone or anything dear reader, except to the glory of the Most High, to His Kingdom, and to our growing relationship with Him.

****

compiled by Miguel A. Valembrun Jr.

In an effort to make this a more user-friendly experience and to honor and distinguish the Lord our God, I took the liberty of highlighting personal and possessive pronouns referring to Christ (except when He refers to Himself). His words are bold and italicized. You will see what I mean shortly.

This book is a guide and resource to promote better understanding of the four Gospels. Therefore, it should be treated as such. It is not guaranteed to be without error. However, by my estimation, at least 97% of the contents were drawn directly from the Gospels. I simply compiled them, added some transitional elements here and there to ensure a seamless read, and finally, minimal commentary. Please use discernment, show grace, and certainly feel free to reach out to me using the following email to inform me if you suspect to have found an error (or errors):

miguelvalembrunjr@gmail.com

Overall, I am quite confident that because of the time I invested in reading the Word, meditating on it frequently, praying often for wisdom and understanding, cross referencing, researching, and testing the spirits along the way, our Heavenly Father has given me a high level of understanding which I have been happy to share in this book.

The Gospel ("Good News from God") was intended to be shared with the world and the better we understand the gospels ("the four books of Matthew, Mark, Luke, and John), the more we can appreciate it. Since all scripture is profitable for doctrine, reproof, and correction, I continue to be a student, submitted to the authority of God and His infallible Word. Therefore again, if you suspect an error, please feel free to share it with me so that we might sharpen each other. No one, except the LORD Himself, is above correction.

May this work, dear reader, be a blessing along your path toward a better understanding of, and relationship with our risen Lord and Savior. He was certainly a unique and special man; the Son of the living God, in whom the fullness of the godhead dwelt bodily. He is the only human being to have ever lived perfectly (without blemish or provable moral failure); the only one to have ever died to atone for the sins of man, and the only human to have ever resurrected by His own power (which is the power of the Father, for He and the Father are one). "There is salvation in no one else, for there is no other name under heaven given to people by which we must be saved." - Acts 4:12

As you read this book, behold your Messiah who came humbly to earth showing the love, compassion, patience, will, and the power of the Heavenly Father. Behold also the other invisible qualities of God which He displayed. It is accurate to say that to know the Son of God is to know the Father since "He is the image of the invisible God." - Colossians 1:15

One final detail. The scriptures that were compiled were almost entirely sourced from the World English Bible translation.

CHAPTER 1

THE BEGINNING

This is the beginning of the Good News of Jesus the Messiah, outlining His origin, genealogy, and manifold deeds. [c.f. Matthew 1:1 & Mark 1:1]

In the beginning was the Word, and the Word was with God, and the Word was God. The same was in the beginning with God. All things were made through Him. Without Him was not anything made that has been made. In Him was life, and the life was the light of men. The light shines in the darkness, and the darkness hasn't overcome it.

He was in the world, and the world was made through Him, and the world didn't recognize Him. He came to His own, and those who were His own didn't receive Him. But as many as received Him, to them He gave the right to become God's children, to those who believe in His name: who were born not of blood, nor of the will of the flesh, nor of the will of man, but of God. The Word became flesh, and lived among us. We saw His glory, such glory as of the one and only Son of the Father, full of grace and truth. John testified about Him. He cried out, saying, "This was He of whom I said, 'He who comes after me has surpassed me, for He was before me.'" From His fullness we all received grace upon grace. For the law was given through Moses. Grace and truth came through Jesus Christ. No one has seen God at any time. The one and only Son, who is in the bosom of the Father, He has declared Him.—[John 1:1-18]

Since many have undertaken to set in order a narrative concerning those matters which have been fulfilled among us, even as those who from the beginning were eyewitnesses and ministers of the word delivered them to us, it seemed good also, having traced the course of all things accurately from the first, to write to you in order, most excellent Lover of God; that you might know the certainty concerning the things in which you were instructed.—[Luke 1:1-4. (Please note: It actually says, "most excellent Theophilus;" which seems to have been a proper name meaning "Lover of God." However, in this

consolidated book, you, dear reader, for all intents and purposes are
Theophilus.)]

ZACHARIAS ENCOUNTERS the ANGEL GABRIEL

There was in the days of Herod, the king of Judea, a certain priest
named Zacharias, of the priestly division of Abijah. He had a wife of
the daughters of Aaron, and her name was Elizabeth. They were both
righteous before God, walking blamelessly in all the commandments
and ordinances of the Lord. But they had no child, because Elizabeth
was barren, and they both were well advanced in years. Now it
happened, while he executed the priest's office before God in the
order of his division, according to the custom of the priest's office,
that his lot was to enter into the temple of the Lord and burn
incense. The whole multitude of the people were praying outside at
the hour of incense.

An angel of the Lord appeared to him, standing on the right side of
the altar of incense. Zacharias was troubled when he saw him, and
fear fell upon him. But the angel said to him, "Don't be afraid,
Zacharias, because your request has been heard, and your wife,
Elizabeth, will bear you a son, and you shall call his name John. You
will have joy and gladness; and many will rejoice at his birth. For he
will be great in the sight of the Lord, and he will drink no wine nor
strong drink. He will be filled with the Holy Spirit, even from his
mother's womb. He will turn many of the children of Israel to the
Lord, their God. He will go before Him in the spirit and power of
Elijah, 'to turn the hearts of the fathers to the children,' and the
disobedient to the wisdom of the just; to make ready a people
prepared for the Lord."

Zacharias said to the angel, "How can I be sure of this? For I am an
old man, and my wife is well advanced in years."

The angel answered him, "I am Gabriel, who stands in the presence
of God. I was sent to speak to you, and to bring you this good news.
Behold, you will be silent and not able to speak, until the day that

these things will happen, because you didn't believe my words, which will be fulfilled in their proper time."

The people were waiting for Zacharias, and they marveled that he delayed in the temple. When he came out, he could not speak to them, and they perceived that he had seen a vision in the temple. He continued making signs to them, and remained mute. It happened, when the days of his service were fulfilled, he departed to his house. After these days Elizabeth, his wife, conceived, and she hid herself five months, saying, "Thus has the Lord done to me in the days in which he looked at me, to take away my reproach among men."—[Luke 1:5-25]

MARY'S ENCOUNTER with the ANGEL GABRIEL

Now in the sixth month, the angel Gabriel was sent from God to a city of Galilee, named Nazareth, to a virgin pledged to be married to a man whose name was Joseph, of the house of David. The virgin's name was Mary. Having come in, the angel said to her, "Rejoice, you highly favored one! The Lord is with you. Blessed are you among women!"

But when she saw him, she was greatly troubled at the saying, and considered what kind of salutation this might be. The angel said to her, "Don't be afraid, Mary, for you have found favor with God. Behold, you will conceive in your womb, and bring forth a son, and will call his name 'Jesus.' He will be great, and will be called the Son of the Most High. The Lord God will give Him the throne of his father, David, and He will reign over the house of Jacob forever. There will be no end to His Kingdom."

Mary said to the angel, "How can this be, seeing I am a virgin?"

The angel answered her, "The Holy Spirit will come on you, and the power of the Most High will overshadow you. **Therefore also** the Holy one who is born from you will be called the Son of God. Behold, Elizabeth, your relative, also has conceived a son in her old age; and this is the sixth month with her who was called barren. For everything spoken by God is possible."

Mary said, "Behold, the handmaid of the Lord; be it to me according to your word."

The angel departed from her. Mary arose in those days and went into the hill country with haste, into a city of Judah, and entered into the house of Zacharias and greeted Elizabeth. It happened, when Elizabeth heard Mary's greeting, that the baby leaped in her womb, and Elizabeth was filled with the Holy Spirit. She called out with a loud voice, and said, "Blessed are you among women, and blessed is the fruit of your womb! Why am I so favored, that the mother of my Lord should come to me? For behold, when the voice of your greeting came into my ears, the baby leaped in my womb for joy! Blessed is she who believed, for there will be a fulfillment of the things which have been spoken to her from the Lord!"

Mary said,

> "My soul magnifies the Lord.
>> My spirit has rejoiced in God my Savior,
>> For He has looked at the humble state of His handmaid.
>
> For behold, from now on, all generations will call me blessed.
>> For He who is mighty has done great things for me.
>> Holy is His name.
>> His mercy is for generations of generations on those who
> fear Him.
>
> He has shown strength with His arm.
>> He has scattered the proud in the imagination of their
> heart.
>
> He has put down princes from their thrones.
>> And has exalted the lowly.

He has filled the hungry with good things.
He has sent the rich away empty.

He has given help to Israel, His servant, that he might remember mercy,
As He spoke to our fathers,
To Abraham and his seed forever."

Mary stayed with her about three months, and then returned to her house. Now the time that Elizabeth should give birth was fulfilled, and she brought forth a son. Her neighbors and her relatives heard that the Lord had magnified His mercy towards her, and they rejoiced with her. It happened on the eighth day, that they came to circumcise the child; and they would have called him Zacharias, after the name of the father. His mother answered, "Not so; but he will be called John."

They said to her, "There is no one among your relatives who is called by this name." They made signs to his father, what he would have him called.

He asked for a writing tablet, and wrote, "His name is John."

They all marveled. His mouth was opened immediately, and his tongue freed, and he spoke, blessing God. Fear came on all who lived around them, and all these sayings were talked about throughout all the hill country of Judea. All who heard them laid them up in their heart, saying, "What then will this child be?" The hand of the Lord was with him. His father, Zacharias, was filled with the Holy Spirit, and prophesied, saying,

"Blessed be the Lord, the God of Israel,
For He has visited and worked redemption for His people;

And has raised up a horn of salvation for us in the house of His servant David
(As He spoke by the mouth of His holy prophets who have been from of old),

Salvation from our enemies, and from the hand of all who hate us;

To show mercy towards our fathers,
   To remember His holy covenant,

The oath which He spoke to Abraham, our father,
   To grant to us that we, being delivered out of the hand of our enemies, should serve Him without fear,
   In holiness and righteousness before Him all the days of our life.

And you, child, will be called a prophet of the Most High,
   For you will go before the face of the Lord to make ready His ways,
   To give knowledge of salvation to His people by the remission of their sins,

Because of the tender mercy of our God,
   Whereby the dawn from on high will visit us,
   To shine on those who sit in darkness and the shadow of death;
   To guide our feet into the way of peace."

The child was growing, and becoming strong in spirit, and was in the desert until the day of his public appearance to Israel.—[Luke 1 (FULL CHAPTER)]

CHAPTER 2

DIVINE PROMISES FULFILLED

The book of the generation of Jesus Christ, the son of David, the son of Abraham.

Abraham begat Isaac; and Isaac begat Jacob; and Jacob begat Judah and his brethren; and Judah begat Perez and Zerah of Tamar; and Perez begat Hezron; and Hezron begat Ram; and Ram begat Amminadab; and Amminadab begat Nahshon; and Nahshon begat Salmon; and Salmon begat Boaz of Rahab; and Boaz begat Obed of Ruth; and Obed begat Jesse; and Jesse begat David the king.

And David begat Solomon of her *that had been the wife* of Uriah; and Solomon begat Rehoboam; and Rehoboam begat Abijah; and Abijah begat Asa; and Asa begat Jehoshaphat; and Jehoshaphat begat Joram; and Joram begat Uzziah; and Uzziah begat Jotham; and Jotham begat Ahaz; and Ahaz begat Hezekiah; and Hezekiah begat Manasseh; and Manasseh begat Amon; and Amon begat Josiah; and Josiah begat Jechoniah and his brethren, at the time of the carrying away to Babylon.

And after the carrying away to Babylon, Jechoniah begat Shealtiel; and Shealtiel begat Zerubbabel; and Zerubbabel begat Abiud; and Abiud begat Eliakim; and Eliakim begat Azor; and Azor begat Sadoc; and Sadoc begat Achim; and Achim begat Eliud; and Eliud begat Eleazar; and Eleazar begat Matthan; and Matthan begat Jacob; and Jacob begat Joseph the husband of Mary, of whom was born Jesus, who is called Christ.

So all the generations from Abraham unto David are fourteen generations; and from David unto the carrying away to Babylon fourteen generations; and from the carrying away to Babylon unto the Christ fourteen generations.

Now the birth of Jesus Christ was on this wise: When his mother Mary had been betrothed to Joseph, before they came together she was found with child of the Holy Spirit. And Joseph, her husband, being a righteous man, and not willing to make her a public example, was minded to put her away privily. But when he thought on these things, behold, an angel of the Lord appeared unto him in a dream, saying, Joseph, you son of David, fear not to take unto yourself Mary as your wife: for that which is conceived in her is of the Holy Spirit. And she shall bring forth a son; and you shall call his name JESUS; for it is he who will save his people from their sins. Now all this will come to pass, that it might be fulfilled which was spoken by the Lord through the prophet, saying,

"Behold, the virgin shall be with child, and shall bring forth a son,

And they shall call his name Immanuel;" (c.f. Isaiah 7:14)

which is, being interpreted, "God with us." And Joseph arose from his sleep, and did as the angel of the Lord commanded him, and took unto him his wife; and knew her not until she had brought forth a son: and he called His name JESUS. —[Matthew 1:1-25 (FULL CHAPTER)]

Now it happened in those days, that a decree went out from Caesar Augustus that all the world should be enrolled (or registered). This was the first enrollment made when Quirinius was governor of Syria. All went to enroll themselves, everyone to his own city. Joseph also went up from Galilee, out of the city of Nazareth, into Judea, to the city of David, which is called Bethlehem, because he was of the house and family of David; to enroll himself with Mary, who was pledged to be married to him as wife, being pregnant.

It happened, while they were there, that the day had come that she should give birth. She brought forth her firstborn son, and she wrapped Him in bands of cloth, and laid Him in a feeding trough, because there was no room for them in the inn. —[Luke 2:1-7]

There were shepherds in the same country staying in the field, and keeping watch by night over their flock. Behold, an angel of the Lord stood by them, and the glory of the Lord shone around them, and they were terrified. The angel said to them, "Don't be afraid, for behold, I bring you good news of great joy which will be to all the people. For there is born to you, this day, in the city of David, a Savior, who is Christ the Lord. This is the sign to you: you will find a baby wrapped in strips of cloth, lying in a feeding trough." Suddenly, there was with the angel a multitude of the heavenly host praising God, and saying,

> "Glory to God in the highest,
>   On earth peace, good will toward men."

It happened, when the angels went away from them into the sky, that the shepherds said one to another, "Let's go to Bethlehem, now, and see this thing that has happened, which the Lord has made known to us." They came with haste, and found both Mary and Joseph, and the baby was lying in the feeding trough. When they saw it, they publicized widely the saying which was spoken to them about this child. All who heard it wondered at the things which were spoken to them by the shepherds. But Mary kept all these sayings, pondering them in her heart. The shepherds returned, glorifying and praising God for all the things that they had heard and seen, just as it was told them. —[Luke 2:8-20]

When eight days were fulfilled for the circumcision of the child, His name was called Jesus, which was given by the angel before He was conceived in the womb.

When the days of their purification according to the law of Moses were fulfilled, they brought Him up to Jerusalem, to present Him to the Lord (as it is written in the law of the Lord, "Every male who opens the womb shall be called holy to the Lord"), and to offer a sacrifice according to that which is said in the law of the Lord, "A pair of turtledoves, or two young pigeons."

Behold, there was a man in Jerusalem whose name was Simeon. This man was righteous and devout, looking for the consolation of Israel, and the Holy Spirit was on him. It had been revealed to him by the Holy Spirit that he should not see death before he had seen the Lord's Christ. He came in the Spirit into the temple. When the parents brought in the child, Jesus, that they might do concerning Him according to the custom of the law, then he received him into his arms, and blessed God, and said,

> "Now you are releasing your servant, Master,
>> According to Your word, in peace;
>
> For my eyes have seen Your salvation,
>> Which You have prepared before the face of all peoples;
>
> A light for revelation to the Gentiles,
>> And the glory of Your people Israel."

Joseph and His mother were marveling at the things which were spoken concerning Him, and Simeon blessed them, and said to Mary, His mother, "Behold, this child is set for the falling and the rising of many in Israel, and for a sign which is spoken against. Yes, a sword will pierce through your own soul, that the thoughts of many hearts may be revealed." —[Luke 2:21-35]

There was one Anna, a prophetess, the daughter of Phanuel, of the tribe of Asher (she was of a great age, having lived with a husband seven years from her virginity, and she had been a widow for about eighty-four years), who didn't depart from the temple, worshiping with fastings and petitions night and day. Coming up at that very hour, she gave thanks to the Lord, and spoke of Him to all those who were looking for redemption in Jerusalem.—[Luke 2:36-38]

WISE MEN VISIT

Now when Jesus was born in Bethlehem of Judaea in the days of Herod the king, behold, Wise-men from the east came to Jerusalem, saying, Where is He that is born King of the Jews? for we saw His star in the east, and came to worship Him. And when Herod the king heard it, he was troubled, and all Jerusalem with him. And gathering together all the chief priests and scribes of the people, he inquired of them where the Christ should be born. And they said unto him, In Bethlehem of Judaea: for thus it is written through the prophet,

"And you Bethlehem, land of Judah,

Are in no wise least among the princes of Judah:

For out of you shall come forth a governor,

Who shall be shepherd of my people Israel." (c.f. Micah 5)

Then Herod privily called the Wise-men, and learned from them exactly what time the star had appeared. And he sent them to Bethlehem, and said, Go and search out exactly concerning the young child; and when you have found Him, bring me word, that I also may come and worship Him. And they, having heard the king, went their way; and lo, the star, which they saw in the east, went before them, till it came and stood over where the young child was. And when they saw the star, they rejoiced with exceeding great joy. —[Matthew 2:1-10]

And the wise men came into the house and saw the young child with Mary His mother; and they fell down and worshiped Him; and opening their treasures they offered unto Him gifts, gold and frankincense and myrrh. And being warned *of God* in a dream that they should not return to Herod, they departed into their own country another way. —[Matthew 2:11-12]

FLIGHT TO EGYPT

Now after the wise men had departed, behold, an angel of the Lord appeared to Joseph in a dream, saying, Arise and take the young child and his mother, and flee into Egypt, and remain there until I tell you: for Herod will seek the young child to destroy Him. And he arose and took the young child and His mother by night, and departed into Egypt; and was there until the death of Herod: that it might be fulfilled which was spoken by the Lord through the prophet, saying, Out of Egypt did I call My Son. —[Matthew 2:13-15]

Then Herod, when he saw that he was tricked by the Wise-men, was exceeding wroth, and sent forth, and slew all the male children that were in Bethlehem, and in all the borders thereof, from two years old and under, according to the time which he had exactly learned of the Wise-men. Then was fulfilled that which was spoken through Jeremiah the prophet, saying,

> "A voice was heard in Ramah,
>
> Weeping and great mourning,
>
> Rachel weeping for her children;
>
> And she would not be comforted, because they are not."

But when Herod was dead, behold, an angel of the Lord appeared in a dream to Joseph in Egypt, saying, "Arise and take the young child and His mother, and go into the land of Israel: for they are dead that sought the young child's life." And he arose and took the young child and His mother, and came into the land of Israel. But when he heard that Archelaus was reigning over Judaea in the room of his father Herod, he was afraid to go there; and being warned *of God* in a dream, he withdrew into the parts of Galilee, and came and dwelt in a city called Nazareth; that it might be fulfilled which was spoken through the prophets, that He should be called a Nazarene.—[Matthew 2:16-23]

When they had accomplished all things that were according to the law of the Lord, they returned into Galilee, to their own city, Nazareth. —[Luke 2:39]

The child was growing, and was becoming strong in spirit, being filled with wisdom, and the grace of God was upon Him. His parents went every year to Jerusalem at the feast of the Passover.

When He was twelve years old, they went up to Jerusalem according to the custom of the feast, and when they had fulfilled the days, as they were returning, the boy Jesus stayed behind in Jerusalem. Joseph and His mother didn't know it, but supposing Him to be in the company, they went a day's journey, and they looked for Him among their relatives and acquaintances. When they didn't find Him, they returned to Jerusalem, looking for Him. It happened after three days they found Him in the temple, sitting in the midst of the teachers, both listening to them, and asking them questions. All who heard Him were amazed at His understanding and His answers. When they saw Him, they were astonished, and His mother said to Him, "Son, why have You treated us this way? Behold, Your father and I were anxiously looking for You."

He said to them, *"Why were you looking for me? Didn't you know that I must be in my Father's house?"* They didn't understand the saying which He spoke to them. And He went down with them, and came to Nazareth. He was subject to them, and His mother kept all these sayings in her heart. And Jesus increased in wisdom and stature, and in favor with God and men.

Now in the fifteenth year of the reign of Tiberius Caesar, Pontius Pilate being governor of Judea, and Herod being tetrarch of Galilee, and his brother Philip tetrarch of the region of Ituraea and Trachonitis, and Lysanias tetrarch of Abilene, in the high priesthood of Annas and Caiaphas, the word of God came to John, the son of Zacharias, in the wilderness. —[Luke 2:40-3:2]

CHAPTER 3

JOHN THE BAPTIST: MESSENGER of GOD

In those days, there came a man sent from God whose name was John. The same came as a witness, that he might testify about the light, that all might believe through Him. He was not the light, but was sent that he might testify about the light. The true light that enlightens everyone was coming into the world. He came preaching in the wilderness of Judea, saying, "Repent for the kingdom of heaven has come near." —[John 1:6-9, Matthew 3:1-2]

(John was the son of Elizabeth and Zacharias who had grown up to be a Baptizer.)

This was the beginning of the Gospel of Jesus Christ, the Son of God. —[Mark 1:1]

As it is written in the prophets,

> "Behold, I send my messenger before Your face,
> Who will prepare Your way before You... This messenger was John who came baptizing in the wilderness and preaching the baptism of repentance for forgiveness of sins. All the country of Judea and all those of Jerusalem went out to him. They were baptized by him in the Jordan river, confessing their sins. —[Mark 1:2-5]

For John was the one who was spoken of by the prophet Isaiah when he said:

> "The voice of one crying in the wilderness,
> 'Make ready the way of the Lord.
>
> Make His paths straight.
> Every valley will be filled.

> Every mountain and hill will be brought low.
> The crooked will become straight,
> And the rough ways smooth.

All flesh will see God's salvation.' —[Matthew 3:3; Mark 1:2-3; Luke 3:4-6]

Now John himself wore clothing made of camel's hair, with a leather belt around his waist and ate locusts and wild honey. —[Matthew 3:4; Mark 1:6]

And he preached saying, "After me comes He who is mightier than I, the strap of whose sandals I am unworthy to stoop down and untie. I have baptized you with water, but He will baptize you with the Holy Spirit. His winnowing fork is in His hand, to clear His threshing floor and to gather the wheat into His barn, but the chaff He will burn with unquenchable fire." So with many other exhortations he preached good news to the people. —[Matthew 3:11-12; Mark 1:7-8; Luke 3:16-18]

At that time, Jerusalem and all Judea and all the region around the Jordan were going out to him, and they were baptized by him in the river Jordan, confessing their sins. *But when he saw many Pharisees and Sadducees coming for his baptism, he said to the multitude of them,* "You offspring of vipers, who warned you to flee from the wrath to come? Therefore bring forth fruit worthy of repentance! Don't think to yourselves, 'We have Abraham for our father,' for I tell you that God is able to raise up children to Abraham from these stones.

> "Even now the axe lies at the root of the trees. Therefore, every tree that doesn't bring forth good fruit is cut down, and cast into the fire. —[Matthew 3:5-10; Luke 3:7-9]

The multitudes asked him, "What then must we do?" —[Luke 3:10]

He answered them, "He who has two coats, let him give to him who has none. He who has food, let him do likewise."

Tax collectors also came to be baptized, and they said to him, "Teacher, what must we do?"

He said to them, "Collect no more than that which is appointed to you."

Soldiers also asked him, saying, "What about us? What must we do?"

He said to them, "Extort from no one by violence, neither accuse anyone wrongfully. Be content with your wages."

As the people were in expectation, and all men reasoned in their hearts concerning John, whether perhaps he was the Christ, John answered them all… "I indeed baptize you in water for repentance, but He who comes after me is mightier than I, whose sandals I am not worthy to carry. He will baptize you in the Holy Spirit. His winnowing fork is in His hand, and He will thoroughly cleanse His threshing floor. He will gather His wheat into the barn, but the chaff He will burn with unquenchable fire."—[Matthew 3:11-12, Luke 3:11-16]

Then Jesus came from Galilee to the Jordan to John, to be baptized by him. But John would have hindered Him, saying, "I need to be baptized by You, and You come to me?"—[Matthew 3:13-14]

THE BAPTISM of JESUS

But Jesus, answering, said to him, *"Allow it now, for this is the fitting way for us to fulfill all righteousness."* Then he allowed him. Jesus, when He was baptized, went up directly from the water: and immediately as He was in prayer, the heavens were opened to

Him. He saw the Spirit of God descending as a dove, and coming on Him. Behold, a voice out of the heavens said, "This is My beloved Son, with whom I am well pleased." —[Matthew 3:15-17; Mark 1:9-11; Luke 3:21-22] *Please note: Mark 1:11 and Luke 3:22 say "You are my beloved Son, in whom I am well pleased." God seems to have spoken with the surrounding audience and Jesus at the same time. For it is possible for people to hear two different messages at the same time, a phenomenon called an "auditory illusion."*

These things were done in Bethany beyond the Jordan, where John was baptizing. —[John 1:28]

THE TEMPTATION of JESUS

Then Jesus, full of the Holy Spirit, was led up by the Spirit from the Jordan into the wilderness to be tempted by the devil. —[Matthew 4:1]

After Jesus had fasted forty days and forty nights, having eaten nothing in that span, He was hungry. The tempter came and said to Him, "If you are the Son of God, command that these stones become bread."

But He answered, *"It is written, 'Man shall not live by bread alone, but by every word that proceeds out of the mouth of God.'"*

Then the devil took Him into the holy city. He set Him on the pinnacle of the temple, and said to Him, "If you are the Son of God, throw Yourself down, for it is written, 'He will give His angels charge concerning you.' and, 'On their hands they will bear you up, So that you don't dash your foot against a stone.'"

Jesus said to him, *"Again, it is written, 'You shall not test the Lord, your God.'"*

Again, the devil took Him to an exceedingly high mountain, and showed Him all the kingdoms of the world, and their glory in a moment. He said to Him, "I will give You all of these things, if You will fall down and worship me. for it has been delivered to me; and I give it to whomever I want."

Then Jesus said to him, *"**Get behind me,** Satan! For it is written, 'You shall worship the Lord your God, and him only shall you serve.'"*

Then the devil left Him, and behold, angels came and ministered to Him.—[Matthew 4:1-11; Luke 4:1-13 and more concisely in Mark 1:12-13]

BEHOLD THE LAMB of GOD

The next day, John the Baptist saw Jesus coming to him, and said, "Behold, the Lamb of God, who takes away the sin of the world! This is He of whom I said, 'After me comes a man who is preferred before me, for He was before me.' I didn't know Him, but for this reason I came baptizing in water: that He would be revealed to Israel." John testified, saying, "I have seen the Spirit descending like a dove out of heaven, and it remained on Him. I didn't recognize Him, but He who sent me to baptize in water, He said to me, 'On whomever you will see the Spirit descending, and remaining on Him, the same is He who baptizes in the Holy Spirit.' I have seen, and have testified that this is the Son of God.

Again, the following day, John was standing with two of his disciples, and he looked at Jesus as He walked, and said, "Behold, the Lamb of God!" The two disciples heard him speak, and they followed Jesus. Jesus turned, and saw them following, and said to them, *"What are you looking for?"*

They said to Him, "Rabbi" (which is to say, being interpreted, Teacher), "where are you staying?"

He said to them, *"Come, and see."*

They came and saw where He was staying, and they stayed with Him that day. It was about the tenth hour. One of the two who heard John, and followed Him, was Andrew, Simon Peter's brother. He first found his own brother, Simon, and said to him, "We have found the Messiah!" (which is, being interpreted, Christ). He brought him to Jesus. Jesus looked at him, and said, *"You are Simon the son of Jonah. You shall be called Cephas"* (which is by interpretation, Peter).

On the next day, He was determined to go out into Galilee. Finding Philip, Jesus said to him, *"Follow me."* Now Philip was from Bethsaida, of the city of Andrew and Peter. Philip found Nathanael, and said to him, "We have found Him, of whom Moses in the law, and the prophets, wrote: Jesus of Nazareth, the son of Joseph."

Nathanael said to him, "Can any good thing come out of Nazareth?"

Philip said to him, "Come and see."

Jesus saw Nathanael coming to Him, and said about him, *"Behold, an Israelite indeed, in whom there is no deceit!"*

Nathanael said to Him, "How do you know me?"

Jesus answered him, *"Before Philip called you, when you were under the fig tree, I saw you."*

Nathanael answered Him, "Rabbi, you are the Son of God! You are King of Israel!"

Jesus answered him, *"Because I told you, 'I saw you underneath the fig tree,' do you believe? You will see greater things than these!"* He said to him, *"Most assuredly, I tell you, hereafter you will see heaven opened, and the angels of God ascending and descending on the Son of Man."* —[John 1:29-51]

CHAPTER 4

THE WEDDING at CANA

Jesus returned in the power of the Spirit into Galilee. —[Luke 4:14]

On the third day, there was a marriage in Cana of Galilee. Jesus' mother was there. Jesus also was invited, with his disciples, to the marriage. When the wine ran out, Jesus' mother said to him, "They have no wine."

Jesus said to her, *"Woman, what does that have to do with you and me? My hour has not yet come."*

His mother said to the servants, "Whatever He says to you, do it." Now there were six water pots of stone set there after the Jews' manner of purifying, containing two or three metretes (1 metrete = 40 litres) apiece. Jesus said to them, *"Fill the water pots with water."* They filled them up to the brim. He said to them, *"Now draw some out, and take it to the ruler of the feast."* So they took it. When the ruler of the feast tasted the water now become wine, and didn't know where it came from (but the servants who had drawn the water knew), the ruler of the feast called the bridegroom, and said to him, "Everyone serves the good wine first, and when the guests have drunk freely, then that which is worse. You have kept the good wine until now!" This was the beginning of the signs Jesus did in Cana of Galilee, and revealed His glory; and His disciples believed in Him.

After this, He went down to Capernaum, with His mother, brothers, and disciples, and they remained there a few days. —[John 2:1-12]

THE 1st CLEANSING OF THE TEMPLE

The Passover of the Jews was at hand, and Jesus went up to Jerusalem. He found in the temple those who sold oxen, sheep, and doves, and the changers of money sitting. He made a whip of cords, and threw all out of the temple, both the sheep and the oxen; and He poured out the changers' money, and overthrew their tables. To those who sold the doves, He said, *"Take these things out of here! Don't make my Father's house a marketplace!"* His disciples remembered that it was written, "Zeal for Your house will eat Me up."

The Jews therefore answered Him, "What sign do You show us, seeing that You do these things?"

Jesus answered them, *"Destroy this temple, and in three days I will raise it up."*

The Jews therefore said, "Forty-six years was this temple in building, and will You raise it up in three days?" But He spoke of the temple of His body. (((When therefore He was raised from the dead, His disciples would remember that He said this, and they would believe the Scripture, and the word which Jesus had said.)))

Now when He was in Jerusalem at the Passover, during the feast, many believed in His name, observing His signs which He did. But Jesus didn't trust Himself to them, because He knew everyone, and because He didn't need for anyone to testify concerning man; for He Himself knew what was in man.—[JOHN 2:13-25]

Now there was a man of the Pharisees named Nicodemus, a ruler of the Jews. The same came to Him by night, and said to Him, "Rabbi, we know that You are a teacher who came from God, for no one can do these signs that You do, unless God is with Him."

Jesus answered him, *"Most assuredly, I tell you, unless one is born anew, he can't see the Kingdom of God."*

Nicodemus said to Him, "How can a man be born when he is old? Can He enter a second time into His mother's womb, and be born?"

Jesus answered, *"Most assuredly I tell you, unless one is born of water and spirit, he can't enter into the Kingdom of God! That which is born of the flesh is flesh. That which is born of the*

Spirit is spirit. Don't marvel that I said to you, 'You must be born anew.' The <u>wind</u> blows where it wants to, and you hear its sound, but don't know where it comes from and where it is going. So is everyone who is born of the Spirit."

Nicodemus answered Him, "How can these things be?"

Jesus answered him, *"Are you the teacher of Israel, and don't understand these things? Most assuredly I tell you, we speak that which we know, and testify of that which we have seen, and you don't receive our witness. If I told you earthly things and you don't believe, how will you believe if I tell you heavenly things? No one has ascended into heaven, but he who descended out of heaven, the Son of Man, who is in heaven. As Moses lifted up the serpent in the wilderness, even so must the Son of Man be lifted up, that whoever believes in him should not perish, but have eternal life. For God so loved the world, that he gave his one and only Son, that whoever believes in him should not perish, but have eternal life. For God didn't send his Son into the world to judge the world, but that the world should be saved through him. He who believes in him is not judged. He who doesn't believe has been judged already, because he has not believed in the name of the one and only Son of God. This is the judgment, that the light has come into the world, and men loved the darkness rather than the light; for their works were evil. For everyone who does evil hates the light, and doesn't come to the light, lest his works would be exposed. But he who does the truth comes to the light, that his works may be revealed, that they have been done in God."*

After these things, Jesus came with His disciples into the land of Judea. He stayed there with them, and baptized. John also was baptizing in Enon near Salim, because there was much water there. People came, and were baptized. For John was not yet thrown into prison. There arose therefore a questioning on the part of John's disciples with some Jews about purification. They came to John, and said to him, "Rabbi, He who was with you beyond the Jordan, to whom you have testified, behold, the same baptizes, and everyone is coming to Him."

John answered, "A man can receive nothing, unless it has been given him from heaven. You yourselves testify that I said, 'I am not the Christ,' but, 'I have been sent before Him.' He who has the bride is the bridegroom; but the friend of the bridegroom, who stands and hears him, rejoices greatly because of the bridegroom's voice. This, my joy, therefore is made full. He must increase, but I must decrease. He who comes from above is above all. He who is from the Earth belongs to the Earth, and speaks of the Earth. He who comes from heaven is above all. What He has seen and heard, of that He testifies; and no one receives His witness. He who has received His witness has set his seal to this, that God is true. For He whom God has sent speaks the words of God; for God gives the Spirit without measure. The Father loves the Son, and has given all things into His hand. One who believes in the Son has eternal life, but one who disobeys the Son won't see life, but the wrath of God remains on him."

When the Lord (Jesus) knew that the Pharisees had heard He was making and baptizing more disciples than John (although Jesus Himself didn't baptize, but His disciples did), He left Judea, and departed into Galilee. He needed to pass through Samaria. So He came to a city of Samaria, called Sychar, near the parcel of ground that Jacob gave to his son, Joseph. Jacob's well was there. Jesus therefore, being tired from His journey, sat down by the well. It was about the sixth hour. A woman of Samaria came to draw water. Jesus said to her, *"Give me a drink."* For His disciples had gone away into the city to buy food.

The Samaritan woman therefore said to Him, "How is it that You, being a Jew, ask for a drink from me, a Samaritan woman?" (For Jews have no dealings with Samaritans.)

Jesus answered her, *"If you knew the gift of God, and who it is who says to you, 'Give me a drink,' you would have asked Him, and He would have given you living water."*

The woman said to Him, "Sir, You have nothing to draw with, and the well is deep. From where then have You that living water? Are You greater than our father, Jacob, who gave us the well, and drank of it himself, as did his children, and his cattle?"

Jesus answered her, *"Everyone who drinks of this water will thirst again, but whoever drinks of the water that I will give him will never thirst again; but the water that I will give him will become in him a well of water springing up to eternal life."*

The woman said to Him, "Sir, give me this water, so that I don't get thirsty, neither come all the way here to draw."

Jesus said to her, *"Go, call your husband, and come here."*

The woman answered, "I have no husband."

Jesus said to her, *"You said well, 'I have no husband,' for you have had five husbands; and he whom you now have is not your husband. This you have said truly."*

The woman said to Him, "Sir, I perceive that You are a prophet. Our fathers worshiped in this mountain, and you Jews say that in Jerusalem is the place where people ought to worship."

Jesus said to her, *"Woman, believe me, the hour comes, when neither in this mountain, nor in Jerusalem, will you worship the Father. You worship that which you don't know. We worship that which we know; for salvation is from the Jews. But the hour comes, and now is, when the true worshippers will worship the Father in spirit and truth, for the Father seeks such to be his worshippers. God is spirit, and those who worship Him must worship in spirit and truth."*

The woman said to Him, "I know that Messiah comes," (He who is called Christ). "When He has come, He will declare to us all things."

Jesus said to her, *"I am He, the one who speaks to you."* At this, His disciples came. They marveled that He was speaking with a woman;

yet no one said, "What are You looking for?" or, "Why do You speak with her?" So the woman left her water pot, and went away into the city, and said to the people, "Come, see a man who told me everything that I did. Can this be the Christ?"

They went out of the city, and were coming to Him. In the meanwhile, the disciples urged Him, saying, "Rabbi, eat."

But He said to them, *"I have food to eat that you don't know about."*

The disciples therefore said one to another, "Has anyone brought Him something to eat?"

Jesus said to them, *"My food is to do the will of Him who sent me, and to accomplish His work. Don't you say, 'There are yet four months until the harvest?' Behold, I tell you, lift up your eyes, and look at the fields, that they are white for harvest already. He who reaps receives wages, and gathers fruit to eternal life; that both he who sows and he who reaps may rejoice together. For in this the saying is true, 'One sows, and another reaps.' I sent you to reap that for which you haven't labored. Others have labored, and you have entered into their labor."*

From that city many of the Samaritans believed in Him because of the word of the woman, who testified, "He told me everything that I did." So when the Samaritans came to Him, they begged Him to stay with them. He stayed there two days. Many more believed because of His word. They said to the woman, "Now we believe, not because of your speaking; for we have heard for ourselves, and know that this is indeed the Christ, the Savior of the world."—[John 2:13-4:42]

CHAPTER 5

JOHN THE BAPTIST ARRESTED

Now Herod, the tetrarch had learned of John the Baptist's ministry and how with many exhortations he preached good news to people. But Herod, who had been reproved by John for Herodias, his brother Philip's wife, and for all the evil things that Herod had done, added this to them all; for John had been saying to him: "It is not lawful for you to have her." Therefore, Herod arrested and imprisoned him. Herod wanted to kill John, but he was afraid of the people because they considered John a prophet. —[Matthew 14:3-5, Mark 6:17-20, and Luke 3:19-20 harmonized]

When Jesus heard that John had been put in prison, he again returned to Galilee (in the power of the Spirit). —[Matthew 4:12, Mark 1:14 and Luke 4:14]

GENEALOGY OF JESUS

Jesus himself was about thirty years of age, being (as was supposed) the son of Joseph, who was the son of Heli, who was the son of Matthat, who descended from Levi, who descended from Melchi, who descended from Janna, as the son of Joseph, who himself was the son of Mattathias, who was the son of Amos, who was the son of Naum, who descended from Esli, who was the son of Nagge, son of Maath, who himself was the son of Mattathias, who was the son of Semei, who was the son of Joseph, who descended from Juda, who was the son of Joanna, who was the son of Rhesa, who himself was the son of Zorobabel, who was the son of Salathiel, who was the son of Neri, who was the son of Melchi, who was the son of Addi, who was the son of Cosam, who himself was the son of Elmodam, who was the son of Er, who was begotten of Jose, which was the son of Eliezer, who himself was the son of Jorim, who descended from Matthat, who was the son of Levi, who was the son of Simeon, who was the son of Juda, who was the son of Joseph, who was the son of Jonan, who descended from Eliakim, who was the son of Melea, who himself was the son of Menan, who was begotten of Mattatha, who was the son of Nathan, who was the son of David, who was the son of Jesse, who was the son of Obed, who himself was the son of Booz, who was the son of Salmon, who was begotten of Naasson, who was the son of Aminadab, who was, in turn, the son of Aram, who was the son of Esrom, who was the son of Phares, the son of Juda, who himself was the son of Jacob, who was the son of Isaac, who was the son of Abraham, who was the son of Thara, who descended from Nachor, who was the son of Saruch, who was the son of Ragau, who was the son of Phalec, begotten of Heber, who was the son of Sala, who descended from Cainan, who was fathered by Arphaxad, who was the son of Sem (Shem), who was the son of Noe (Noah), who was the son of Lamech, who in turn was the son of Mathusala, who was the son of Enoch, who was begotten of Jared, who was the son of Maleleel, who was the son of Cainan, who was the son of Enos, who was the son of Seth, who was the son of Adam, who himself was the son of God.—[Luke 3:23-38]

REJECTED AT NAZARETH

Jesus came to Nazareth, where He had been brought up. He entered, as was His custom, into the synagogue on the Sabbath day, and stood up to read. The book of the prophet Isaiah was handed to Him. He opened the book, and found the place where it was written,

"The Spirit of the Lord is on me,
Because He has anointed me to preach good news to the poor.

He has sent me to heal the brokenhearted,
To proclaim release to the captives,
Recovering of sight to the blind,
To deliver those who are crushed,
And to proclaim the acceptable year of the Lord."

He closed the book, gave it back to the attendant, and sat down. The eyes of all in the synagogue were fastened on Him. He began to tell them, *"Today, this Scripture has been fulfilled in your hearing."*

All testified about Him, and wondered at the gracious words which proceeded out of His mouth, and they said, "Isn't this Joseph's son?"

He said to them, *"Doubtless you will tell me this parable, 'Physician, heal yourself! Whatever we have heard done at Capernaum, do also here in Your hometown.'"* He said, *"Most assuredly I tell you, no prophet is acceptable in his hometown. But truly I tell you, there were many widows in Israel in the days of Elijah, when the sky was shut up three years and six months, when a great famine came over all the land. Elijah was sent to none of them, except to Zarephath, in the land of Sidon, to a woman who was a widow. There were many lepers in Israel in the time of Elisha the prophet, yet not one of them was cleansed, except Naaman, the Syrian."*

They were all filled with wrath in the synagogue, as they heard these things. They rose up, threw Him out of the city, and led Him to the brow of the hill that their city was built on, that they might throw Him off the cliff. But He, passing (miraculously) through the midst of them, went His way as He marveled at their disbelief. He went about among the villages to teach. —[Mark, 6:1-6, Luke 4:16-30]

CHAPTER 6

RETURNING to GALILEE

After the two days He went out from there and went into Galilee. For Jesus Himself testified that a prophet has no honor in his own country. So when He came into Galilee, the Galileans received Him, having seen all the things that He did in Jerusalem at the feast, for they also went to the feast. Jesus came therefore again to Cana of Galilee, where He earlier had made the water into wine. There was a certain nobleman whose son was sick at Capernaum. When he heard that Jesus had come out of Judea into Galilee, he went to Him, and begged Him that He would come down and heal his son, for he was at the point of death. Jesus therefore said to him, *"Unless you see signs and wonders, you will in no way believe."*

The nobleman said to Him, "Sir, come down before my child dies." Jesus said to him, *"Go your way. Your son lives."* The man believed the word that Jesus spoke to him, and he went his way. As he was now going down, his servants met him and reported, saying "Your child lives!" So he inquired of them the hour when he began to get better. They said therefore to him, "Yesterday at the seventh hour, the fever left him." So the father knew that it was at that hour in which Jesus said to him, *"Your son lives."* He believed, as did his whole house. This is again the second sign that Jesus did, having come out of Judea into Galilee.—[John 4:43-54]

THE LAME MAN at the POOL

After these things, there was a feast of the Jews, and Jesus went up to Jerusalem. Now in Jerusalem by the sheep gate, there is a pool, which is called in Hebrew, "Bethesda," having five porches. In these lay a great multitude of those who were sick, blind, lame, or paralyzed, waiting for the moving of the water; for an angel of the Lord went down at certain times into the pool, and stirred up the water.

Whoever stepped in first after the stirring of the water was made whole of whatever disease he had. A certain man was there, who had been sick for thirty-eight years. When Jesus saw him lying there, and knew that he had been sick for a long time, He asked him, *"Do you want to be made well?"*

The sick man answered Him, "Sir, I have no one to put me into the pool when the water is stirred up, but while I'm coming, another steps down before me." Jesus said to Him, *"Arise, take up your mat, and walk."* Immediately, the man was made well, and took up his mat and walked. Now it was the Sabbath on that day. So the Jews said to him who was cured, "It is the Sabbath. It is not lawful for you to carry the mat." He answered them, "He who made me well, the same said to me, *'Take up your mat, and walk.'"*

Then they asked him, "Who is the man who said to you, 'Take up your mat, and walk'?" But he who was healed didn't know who it was, for Jesus had withdrawn, a crowd being in the place. Afterward Jesus found him in the temple, and said to him, *"Behold, you are made well. Sin no more, so that nothing worse happens to you."*

The man went away, and told the Jews that it was Jesus who had made him well. For this cause the Jews persecuted Jesus, and sought to kill Him, because He did these things on the Sabbath. But Jesus answered them, *"My Father is still working, so I am working, too."* For this cause therefore the Jews sought all the more to kill Him, because He not only broke the Sabbath, but also called God His own Father, making Himself equal with God. Jesus therefore answered them, *"Most assuredly, I tell you, the Son can do nothing of Himself, but what He sees the Father doing. For whatever things He does, these the Son also does likewise. For the Father has affection for the Son, and shows Him all things that He Himself does. He will show Him greater works than these, that you may marvel. For as the Father raises the dead and gives them life, even so the Son also gives life to whom He desires. For the Father judges no one, but He has given all judgment to the Son, that all may honor the Son, even as they* honor the Father. He who doesn't honor the Son doesn't honor the Father who sent Him.

"Most assuredly I tell you, he who hears my word, and believes Him who sent me, has eternal life, and doesn't come into judgment, but has passed out of death into life. Most assuredly, I tell you, the hour comes, and now is, when the dead will hear the Son of God's voice; and those who hear will live. For as the Father has life in Himself, even so He gave to the Son also to have life in Himself. He also gave Him authority to execute judgment, because He is a son of man. Don't marvel at this, for the hour comes, in which all that are in the tombs will hear His voice, and will come out; those who have done good, to the resurrection of life; and those who have done evil, to the resurrection of judgment. I can of myself do nothing. As I hear, I judge, and my judgment is righteous; because I don't seek my own will, but the will of my Father who sent me.

"If I testify about myself, my witness is not valid. It is another who testifies about me. I know that the testimony which He testifies about me is true. You have sent to John, and he has testified to the truth. But the testimony which I receive is not from man. However, I say these things that you may be saved. He was the burning and shining lamp, and you were willing to rejoice for a while in his light. But the testimony which I have is greater than that of John, for the works which the Father gave me to accomplish, the very works that I do, testify about me, that the Father has sent me. The Father Himself, who sent me, has testified about me. You have neither heard His voice at any time, nor seen His form. You don't have His word living in you; because you don't believe Him whom He sent.

"You search the Scriptures, because you think that in them you have eternal life; and these are they which testify about me. Yet you will not come to me, that you may have life. I don't receive glory from men. But I know you, that you don't have God's love in yourselves. I have come in my Father's name, and you don't receive me. If another comes in his own name, you will receive *him. How can you believe, who receive glory from one another, and you don't seek the glory that comes from the only God?*

"Don't think that I will accuse you to the Father. There is one who accuses you, even Moses, on whom you have set your hope. For if you believed Moses, you would believe me; for he wrote about me. But if you don't believe his writings, how will you believe my words?" —[John 5:1-44]

FROM NAZARETH TO CAPERNAUM

Leaving Nazareth, He went and lived in Capernaum (in Galilee) by the sea to fulfill what was said through the prophet Isaiah:

"Land of Zebulun and land of Naphtali, the Way of the Sea, beyond the Jordan, Galilee of the Gentiles–the people living in darkness have seen a great light; on those living in the land of the shadow of death a light has dawned."

Proclaiming the good news of God from then on, He said such things as "Repent! The time is fulfilled, and the kingdom of God is at hand! Repent and believe in the gospel." He also taught the people of Capernaum on the sabbath days. News of Him spread throughout the surrounding country. And He taught in their synagogues being glorified by all. —[Matthew 4:13-17, Mark 1:14-15, harmonized with Luke 4:31-32]

JESUS CALLS HIS FIRST DISCIPLES

While Jesus was walking by the lake of Gennesaret (large enough that it is also known as "the Sea of Galilee"), a crowd began to follow Him. He saw two boats on the sea and in one Simon and Andrew, his brother. They had cast a net into the sea, for they were fishermen. (You may recall this Simon whom Jesus had also called "Cephas" meaning the name "Peter"...which itself also means "rock.")

As the multitude began to press in on Jesus to hear the word of God, He boarded the boat belonging to Simon (Peter) and Andrew and asked them to put out a little from the land. Jesus sat down and taught the multitude from the boat. After He had finished speaking, He instructed Simon "Go out further into the deep and let down your nets for a catch." And Simon answered, "Master, we toiled all night and did not catch anything! But at Your word, I will let down the nets." When they had done this, they enclosed a large number of fish, and their nets were breaking. So they signaled to their partners in the other boat to come and help them. Their partners were also brothers by the names of James and John, and their father Zebedee was also on the boat. They came and filled both boats, so that they began to sink.

When Simon Peter saw it, he fell at Jesus' knees and said, "Depart from me, O Lord, for I am a sinful man." For he and all who were with him were astonished at the catch of fish they had taken, including James and John. Jesus replied to Simon saying, "Do not be afraid. Follow me; and from now on, you will be fishers of men." When they had brought their boats to land, Simon, Andrew, James, and John immediately left their boats with Zebedee and their team of hired servants, and they followed Jesus. —[Matthew 4:18-22 and Mark 1:16-20 *harmonized with* Luke 5:1-11]

They (Jesus and his disciples) went into Capernaum, a city of Galilee, and on the Sabbath day He entered into the synagogue with them and taught them. They were astonished at His teaching, for He taught them as one having authority, and not as the scribes. Suddenly, a man in their synagogue who had an unclean spirit cried out loudly, "Ha! What have you to do with us, Jesus of Nazareth? Have you come to destroy us? I know who you are, the Holy One of God." Jesus rebuked, saying, *"Silence! Come out of him!"* Then, the unclean spirit convulsed in the man, throwing him down in their midst while crying boisterously, and it came out of him having done no harm. They were all amazed and questioned among themselves asking, "What is this? A new teaching with authority! He even commands the unclean spirits with authority and power, and they obey." At

once, His fame spread everywhere within the surrounding region of
Galilee. —[Mark 1:21-28 and Luke 4:31-37]

CHAPTER 7

HEALING PETER'S MOTHER IN LAW

Soon after they had come out of the synagogue, they came into the house of Simon and Andrew, with James and John. Now Simon's mother in law lay sick with a fever, and immediately they told Jesus about her. He came and took her by the hand, and raised her up. The fever left her, and she served them. At evening, when the sun had set, they brought to Him all who were sick, and those who were possessed by demons. All the city was gathered together at the door. He healed many who were sick with various diseases, and cast out many demons. He didn't allow the demons to speak, because they knew Him. This was to fulfill what Isaiah the prophet had spoken when he said: "He took our illnesses and bore our diseases."—[Matthew 8:14-17, Mark 1:29-34, Luke 4:38-41 harmonized]

Early in the morning while it was still dark, He rose up and went out, and departed into a deserted place, and prayed there. Simon and those who were with him followed after him; and they found Jesus, and told Him, "Everyone is looking for You." And the people sought Him and came to Him, and would have kept Him from leaving them, but He said to them, *"Let us go elsewhere into the next towns, that I may preach there also, because for this reason I came forth, having been sent for this purpose."* And He went throughout all Galilee and Judea, teaching in their synagogues and proclaiming the gospel of the Kingdom and healing every disease and affliction among the people. So He was glorified by all and His fame spread throughout all Syria, and they brought Him all who were sick with various illnesses, afflicted with pains, demonically oppressed, epileptic, paralytics, and He healed them. And multitudes followed Him from Galilee and the Decapolis, and from Jerusalem, Judea, and beyond the Jordan.—[Matthew 4:23-25, Mark 1:35-39, and Luke 4:42-44 harmonized]

CLEANSING A LEPER

It happened, while He was in one of the cities, behold, there was a man full of leprosy. When the man saw Jesus, he fell on his face, and begged Him, saying, "Lord, if you want to, You can make me clean." Being moved with compassion, Jesus stretched out His hand, and touched him, saying, *"I want to. Be made clean."* Immediately the leprosy left him and he was cleansed. Jesus commanded him saying, *"See that you tell nobody, but go your way, show yourself to the priest, and offer the gift that Moses commanded, as a testimony to them."* But he went out, and began to proclaim it much, and to spread about the matter, so that Jesus could no more openly enter into a city, but was outside in desert places praying. The report concerning Him spread much more, and great multitudes came together from everywhere to hear, and to be healed (by Him) of their infirmities. —[Matthew 8:1-4, Mark 1:40-45, and Luke 5:12-16]

PARALYTIC HEALED

Jesus entered a boat, crossed over, and came into His own city, Capernaum. It was heard that He was in the house, and immediately many gathered together, so that there was no more room, not even around the door. Jesus began speaking the word to them and as He taught, Pharisees and teachers of the law sat by, who had come out of every village of Galilee, Judea, and Jerusalem. The power of the Lord was with Jesus to heal.

Behold, four men carried a paralyzed man on a mat, and sought to bring him in to lay before Jesus. When they could not come near Him on account of the crowd, they went up to the housetop, removed the roof tiles where He was, and lowered the paralyzed man through the opening in the tiles as he lay on his cot. The man descended into the midst before Jesus.

Seeing their faith, Jesus said to the paralytic, *"Son, cheer up! Your sins are forgiven you."*

Then the scribes and Pharisees sitting there, reasoned in their hearts, "This man blasphemes. Who is this that speaks blasphemies? Who can forgive sins but God alone?"

Immediately, Jesus, who had perceived in His Spirit that they so reasoned within themselves, said to them, *"Why do you think evil and reason these things in your hearts? Which is easier, to say, 'Your sins are forgiven;' or to say, 'Get up, and walk?' But that you may know that the Son of Man has authority on earth to forgive sins..." (He said to the paralytic), "I tell you, get up, take up your mat, and go to your house."*

Immediately the paralyzed man rose up before them, took up that which he was lying on, and went out in front of them all, glorifying God. He departed to his house. When the multitudes saw it, they were all amazed, and glorified God, who had given such authority to men. They were filled with fear, saying, "We never saw anything like this!" and "We have seen strange things today."—[Matthew 9:1-8, Mark 2:1-12, and Luke 5:17-28 harmonized]

JESUS CALLS LEVI (after the Paralytic is healed)

After these things He went out, and saw a tax collector named Levi sitting at the tax office, and said to him, "Follow me!"

Levi (also known as Matthew) left everything, and rose up and followed Him. He made a great feast for Jesus in his house. There was a great crowd of tax collectors and others who were reclining with them. The Pharisees and their scribes murmured against Him and His disciples, saying, "Why do You eat and drink with the tax collectors and sinners?" Jesus answered them, *"Those who are healthy have no need for a physician, but those who are sick do. I have not come to call the righteous, but sinners to repentance. But you go and learn what this means: 'I desire mercy, and not sacrifice,' for I came not to call the righteous, but sinners to repentance."*—[Matthew 9:9-14, Mark 2:13-17, and Luke 5:27-32]

Now John's disciples and the Pharisees were fasting. And John the Baptist's disciples came and said to Him, "Why do John's disciples often fast and pray, likewise also the disciples of the Pharisees, but Yours eat and drink?"

He said to them, *"Can you make the friends of the bridegroom fast, while the bridegroom is with them? But the days will come when the bridegroom will be taken away from them. Then they will fast in those days."* He also told a parable to them. *"No one puts a piece from a new garment on an old garment, or else he will tear the new, and also the piece from the new will not match the old. No one puts new wine into old wineskins, or else the new wine will burst the skins, and it will be spilled, and the skins will be destroyed. But new wine must be put into fresh wineskins, and both are preserved. No man having drunk old wine immediately desires new, for he says, 'The old is better.'"*—[Matthew 9:14-17, Mark 2:18-22, and Luke 5:33-39 harmonized]**

LORD OF THE SABBATH:

(MATT 12:1-8, MARK 2:123-28, LUKE 6:1-8)

The second Sabbath, Jesus was going through the grainfields, and His disciples were hungry. As they walked, they began to pick some heads of grain, rubbed them in their hands, and ate the kernels. When the Pharisees saw this, they said to Him, "Look, why are they doing what is unlawful on the Sabbath?"

Jesus answered them, *"Have you never read what David did when he and his companions were hungry and in need? He entered the house of God, and he and his companions ate the consecrated bread—which was not lawful for them to do, but only for the priests. Or haven't you read in the Law that on the Sabbath the priests in the temple desecrate the day and yet are innocent? I tell you that something greater than the temple is here.*

And He said to them, *"The Sabbath was made for man, not man for the Sabbath. So the Son of Man is Lord even of the Sabbath. If you had known what these words mean, 'I desire mercy, not sacrifice,' you would not have condemned the innocent. For the Son of Man is Lord of the Sabbath."*—[Matthew 12:1-8, Mark 2:23-28 and Luke 6:1-5 harmonized]

MAN with the WITHERED HAND

He departed there, and it also happened on another Sabbath that He went into their synagogue and taught. And behold there was a man with a withered right hand. The scribes and Pharisees watched Him, to see whether He would heal on the Sabbath, that they might find an accusation against Him. They asked Him, "Is it lawful to heal on the Sabbath day?" that they might accuse Him. But He knew their thoughts; and He said to the man who had the withered hand, *"Rise up, and stand in the middle."* He arose and stood. Then Jesus said to them, *"I will ask you something: Is it lawful on the Sabbath to do good, or to do harm? To save a life, or to kill? What man is there among you, who has one sheep, and if this one falls into a pit on the Sabbath day, won't he grab on to it, and lift it out? Of how much more value then is a man than a sheep! Therefore it is lawful to do good on the Sabbath day."* He looked around at them all, and said to the man, *"Stretch out your hand."* He did, and his hand was restored as sound as the other.

The Pharisees went out and immediately held counsel with the Herodians against Him, *how to destroy* Him. They were filled with rage, and talked with one another about what they might do to Him. Jesus, perceiving that, withdrew from there (with His disciples) to the sea. —[Matthew 12:9-14, Mark 3:1-6 and Luke 6:6-11 harmonized]

HEALING A BLIND AND MUTE MAN

Great multitudes followed Him from Galilee, Judea, Jerusalem, Idumea, even from beyond the Jordan, and the vicinity of Tyre and Sidon. A great number followed Him who had heard everything that He was doing; and He healed them all, and charged them that they should not make Him known: that it might be fulfilled which was spoken through Isaiah the prophet, saying,

"Behold, my servant whom I have chosen;
   My beloved in whom my soul is well pleased:

I will put my Spirit on him.
   He will proclaim justice to the Gentiles.

He will not strive, nor shout;
   Neither will anyone hear His voice in the streets.

He won't break a bruised reed.
   He won't quench a smoking flax,

Until He leads justice to victory.
   In His name, the Gentiles will hope."

Jesus told His disciples to see that a boat would be ready for Him because of the masses, so that they would not crowd Him; For He had healed many, with the result that all those who had diseases pushed in around Him in order to touch Him, and whenever the unclean spirit saw Him, they would fall down before Him and shout, you are the Son of God! And He strongly warned them not to reveal who He was."

Then, He went home and the multitude gathered again, so that He and His disciples could not even eat. —[Matthew 12:15-21, Mark 3:7-12]

PLENTIFUL HARVEST with FEW LABORERS

Jesus went about all the cities and the villages, teaching in their synagogues and preaching the Good News of the Kingdom, and healing every disease and every sickness among the people. [36] But when He saw the multitudes, He was moved with compassion for them because they were harassed and scattered, like sheep without a shepherd. [37] Then He said to his disciples, *"The harvest indeed is plentiful, but the laborers are few. [38] Pray therefore that the Lord of the harvest will send out laborers into his harvest."*—[Matthew 9:35-38]

THE 12 APOSTLES

Seeing the multitude Jesus went up to the mountain [Mat5:1] to pray, spending the entire night in prayer. When it was day, He called to Himself all those whom He desired from His disciples, and when He had sat down, they came to Him. From among His disciples, He chose twelve to be with Him; twelve whom He named apostles, to be sent out to preach, and to have authority to heal sicknesses and cast out demons.

Here were the twelve appointed:

- Simon, whom He named "Cephas" (meaning Peter when interpreted)
- Andrew, Peter's brother
- James, the son of Zebedee
- and John, the brother of James (both of whom He surnamed "Boanerges," which means "Sons of Thunder")
- Philip
- Bartholomew
- Matthew
- Thomas
- James, the son of Alphaeus
- Thaddaeus (also known as Judas and Jude, the son of James)
- Simon, who was called the Zealot

and

- Judas Iscariot, who also became a traitor

Jesus came down with them, and stood on a level place, with a crowd of his disciples, and a great number of the people from all Judea and Jerusalem, and the sea coast of Tyre and Sidon, who came to hear Him and to be healed of their diseases; as well as those who were troubled by unclean spirits, and they were being healed. All the multitude sought to touch Him, for power came out from Him and healed them all. —[Matthew 10:1-4, Mark 3:13-19, Luke 6:12-19]

CHAPTER 8

THE SERMON ON THE MOUNT

[MATTHEW 4:23-7:29]

Then, He **_lifted up his eyes on his disciples and_** opened his mouth and taught them, saying,

"Blessed are <u>you who are</u> the poor in spirit,
   For <u>yours</u> is the Kingdom of Heaven.

Blessed are those who mourn,
   For they shall be comforted.

Blessed are the gentle,
   For they shall inherit the earth.

Blessed are those who hunger and thirst after righteousness,
   For they shall be filled.

<u>*Blessed are you who weep now, for you shall laugh.*</u>

Blessed are the merciful,
   For they shall obtain mercy.

Blessed are the pure in heart,
   For they shall see God.

Blessed are the peacemakers,
   For they shall be called children of God.

Blessed are those who have been persecuted for righteousness' sake,
   For theirs is the Kingdom of Heaven.

"Blessed are you when people reproach you, <u>hate you,</u> persecute you, <u>exclude you,</u> and say all kinds of evil against you falsely, for my sake. Rejoice <u>in that day, leap for joy,</u> and be exceedingly glad, for great is your reward in heaven. For that is how they

persecuted the prophets who were before you.—[Matthew 5:1-12 and Luke 6:20-23 harmonized]**

But woe to you who are rich, for you have received your consolation. Woe to you who are full now, for you shall be hungry. Woe to you who laugh now, for you shall mourn and weep. Woe to you, when all people speak well of you, for so their fathers did to the false prophets.—[Luke 6:24-26]

"You are the salt of the earth, but if the salt has lost its flavor, with what will it be salted? It is then good for nothing, but to be cast out and trodden under the feet of men. You are the light of the world. A city located on a hill can't be hidden. Neither do you light a lamp, and put it under a measuring basket, but on a stand; and it shines to all who are in the house. Even so, let your light shine before men; that they may see your good works, and glorify your Father who is in heaven.—[Matthew 5:13-16, Mark 4:21-25, Luke 8:16-18]

"Don't think that I came to destroy the law or the prophets. I didn't come to destroy, but to fulfill. For most assuredly, I tell you, until heaven and earth pass away, not even one <u>smallest letter</u> or one <u>tiny pen stroke</u> shall in any way pass away from the law, until all things are accomplished. Whoever, therefore, shall break one of these least commandments, and teach others to do so, shall be called least in the Kingdom of Heaven; but whoever shall do and teach them shall be called great in the Kingdom of Heaven. For I tell you that unless your righteousness exceeds that of the scribes and Pharisees, there is no way you will enter into the Kingdom of Heaven.

"You have heard that it was said to the ancient ones, 'You shall not murder;' and 'Whoever shall murder shall be in danger of the judgment.' But I tell you, that everyone who is angry with his brother without a cause shall be in danger of the judgment; and whoever shall say to his brother, '<u>Raca</u>!' shall be in danger of the council; and whoever shall say, 'You fool!' shall be in danger of the fire of <u>Gehenna</u>.

"If therefore you are offering your gift at the altar, and there remember that your brother has anything against you, leave your gift there before the altar, and go your way. First be reconciled to your brother, and then come and offer your gift. Agree with your adversary quickly, while you are with him in the way; lest perhaps the prosecutor deliver you to the judge, and the judge deliver you to the officer, and you be cast into prison. Most assuredly I tell you, you shall by no means get out of there, until you have paid the last penny.

"You have heard that it was said, ⁻ 'You shall not commit adultery;' but I tell you that everyone who gazes at a woman to lust after her has committed adultery with her already in his heart. If your right eye causes you to stumble, pluck it out and throw it away from you. For it is more profitable for you that one of your members should perish, than for your whole body to be cast into Gehenna. If your right hand causes you to stumble, cut it off, and throw it away from you: for it is profitable for you that one of your members should perish, and not your whole body be thrown into Gehenna.

"It was also said, 'Whoever shall put away his wife, let him give her a writing of divorce,' but I tell you that whoever puts away his wife, except for the cause of sexual immorality, makes her an adulteress; and whoever marries her when she is put away commits adultery.

"Again you have heard that it was said to them of old time, 'You shall not make false vows, but shall perform to the Lord your vows,' but I tell you, don't swear at all: neither by heaven, for it is the throne of God; nor by the earth, for it is the footstool of His feet; nor by Jerusalem, for it is the city of the Great King. Neither shall you swear by your head, for you can't make one hair white or black. But let your 'Yes' be 'Yes' and your 'No' be 'no.' Whatever is more than these is of the evil one.

"You have heard that it was said, 'An eye for an eye, and a tooth for a tooth.' But I tell you, don't resist him who is evil; but

whoever strikes you on your right cheek, turn to him the other also. If anyone sues you to take away your coat, let him have your cloak also. Whoever compels you to go one mile, go with him two. Give to him who asks you, and don't turn away him who desires to borrow from you.

**"You have heard that it was said, 'You shall love your neighbor, and hate your enemy.' But I tell you, love your enemies, bless those who curse you, do good to those who hate you, and pray for those who <u>abuse you,</u> mistreat you and persecute you, that you may be children of your Father who is in heaven. <u>To one who strikes you on the cheek, offer the other also and from one who takes away your cloak, do not withhold your tunic (or shirt) either. Give to everyone who begs from you and from one who takes away your goods do not demand them back. And as you wish that others would do to you, do so to them.</u> For He (the LORD God) makes His sun to rise on the evil and the good, and sends rain on the just and the unjust. For if you love those who love you, <u>what benefit is that to you?</u> What reward do you have? <u>For even sinners love those who love them.</u>

Don't even the tax collectors do the same? If you only greet your friends, what more do you do than others? Don't even the tax collectors do the same? Therefore you shall be perfect, just as your Father in heaven is perfect.**

"Be careful that you don't do your charitable giving before men, to be seen by them, or else you have no reward from your Father who is in heaven. Therefore when you do merciful deeds, don't sound a trumpet before yourself, as the hypocrites do in the synagogues and in the streets, that they may get glory from men. Most assuredly I tell you, they have received their reward. But when you do merciful deeds, don't let your left hand know what your right hand does, so that your merciful deeds may be in secret, then your Father who sees in secret will reward you openly. <u>And if you lend to those from whom you expect to receive, what credit is that to you? Even sinners lend to sinners, to get back the same amount. But love your enemies, and do</u>

good, and lend, expecting nothing in return, and your reward will be great, and you will be children of the Most High, for He is kind to the ungrateful and the evil. Be merciful, even as your Father is merciful. —[Matthew 6:1-6:4 and Luke 6:20-36 harmonized]**

"When you pray, you shall not be as the hypocrites, for they love to stand and pray in the synagogues and in the corners of the streets, that they may be seen by men. Most assuredly, I tell you, they have received their reward. But you, when you pray, enter into your inner chamber, and having shut your door, pray to your Father who is in secret, and your Father who sees in secret will reward you openly. In praying, don't use vain repetitions, as the Gentiles do; for they think that they will be heard for their much speaking. Therefore don't be like them, for your Father knows what things you need, before you ask him. Pray like this: 'Our Father in heaven, may Your name be kept holy. Let Your Kingdom come. Let Your will be done, as in heaven, so on earth. Give us today our daily bread. Forgive us our debts, as we also forgive our debtors. Bring us not into temptation, but deliver us from the evil one. For Yours is the Kingdom, the power, and the glory forever. Amen.'

"For if you forgive men their trespasses, your heavenly Father will also forgive you. But if you don't forgive men their trespasses, neither will your Father forgive your trespasses.

"Moreover when you fast, don't be like the hypocrites, with sad faces. For they disfigure their faces, that they may be seen by men to be fasting. Most assuredly I tell you, they have received their reward. But you, when you fast, anoint your head, and wash your face; so that you are not seen by men to be fasting, but by your Father who is in secret, and your Father, who sees in secret, will reward you.

"Don't lay up treasures for yourselves on the earth, where moth and rust consume, and where thieves break through and steal; but lay up for yourselves treasures in heaven, where neither

moth nor rust consume, and where thieves don't break through and steal; for where your treasure is, there your heart will be also.

"The lamp of the body is the eye. If therefore your eye is sound, your whole body will be full of light. But if your eye is evil, your whole body will be full of darkness. If therefore the light that is in you is darkness, how great is the darkness!

"No one can serve two masters, for either he will hate the one and love the other; or else he will be devoted to one and despise the other. You can't serve both God and Mammon. Therefore, I tell you, don't be anxious for your life: what you will eat, or what you will drink; nor yet for your body, what you will wear. Isn't life more than food, and the body more than clothing? See the birds of the sky, that they don't sow, neither do they reap, nor gather into barns. Your heavenly Father feeds them. Aren't you of much more value than they?

"Which of you, by being anxious, can add one cubit to the measure of his life? Why are you anxious about clothing? Consider the lilies of the field, how they grow. They don't toil, neither do they spin, yet I tell you that even Solomon in all his glory was not dressed like one of these. But if God so clothes the grass of the field, which today exists, and tomorrow is thrown into the oven, won't He much more clothe you, you of little faith?

"Therefore don't be anxious, saying, 'What will we eat?', 'What will we drink?' or, 'With what will we be clothed?' For the Gentiles seek after all these things, for your heavenly Father knows that you need all these things. But seek first God's Kingdom, and His righteousness; and all these things will be given to you as well. Therefore don't be anxious for tomorrow, for tomorrow will be anxious for itself. Each day's own evil is sufficient.

**"Don't judge, so that you won't be judged. _Condemn not, and you will not be condemned; forgive, and you will be forgiven;_

give, and it will be given to you. Good measure, pressed down, shaken together, running over, will be put into your lap. For with whatever judgment you judge, you will be judged; and with whatever measure you measure, it will be measured to you. Can a blind man lead a blind man? Will they not both fall into a pit? A disciple is not above his teacher, but everyone who is fully trained will be like his teacher. Why do you see the speck that is in your brother's eye, but don't consider the beam that is in your own eye? Or how will you tell your brother, 'Let me remove the speck from your eye;' and behold, the beam is in your own eye? You hypocrite! First remove the beam out of your own eye, and then you can see clearly to remove the speck out of your brother's eye. "Don't give that which is holy to the dogs, neither throw your pearls before the pigs, lest perhaps they trample them under their feet, and turn and tear you to pieces.—[Matthew 6:5-7:1-6 and Luke 6:37-42 harmonized]**

"Ask, and it will be given you. Seek, and you will find. Knock, and it will be opened for you. For everyone who asks receives. He who seeks finds. To him who knocks it will be opened. Or who is there among you, who, if his son asks him for bread, will give him a stone? Or if he asks for a fish, who will give him a serpent? If you then, being evil, know how to give good gifts to your children, how much more will your Father who is in heaven give good things to those who ask him! Therefore whatever you desire for men to do to you, you shall also do to them; for this is the law and the prophets.

"Enter in by the narrow gate; for wide is the gate and broad is the way that leads to destruction, and many are those who enter in by it. How narrow is the gate, and restricted is the way that leads to life! Few are those who find it.

*** "Beware of false prophets, who come to you in sheep's clothing, but inwardly are ravening wolves. By their fruits you will know them, as each tree is known by its own fruit. For figs are not gathered from thornbushes, nor grapes from bramble bushes. Even so, every good tree produces good fruit; but the* *corrupt tree produces evil fruit. A good tree can't produce evil fruit, neither can a corrupt tree produce good fruit; Every tree that doesn't grow good fruit is cut down, and thrown into the fire. Therefore, by their fruits you will know them. Not everyone who says to me, 'Lord, Lord,' will enter into the Kingdom of Heaven; but he who does the will of my Father who is in heaven. Many will tell me in that day, 'Lord, Lord, didn't we prophesy in Your name, in Your name cast out demons, and in Your name do many mighty works?' Then I will tell them, 'I never knew you. Depart from me, you who work iniquity.'*—[Matthew 7:15-23 and Luke 6:43-45 harmonized]**

**<u>Why do You call me Lord, Lord, and not do what I tell you?</u>
"Everyone therefore who hears these words of mine, and does them, I will liken him to a wise man, who built his house on a rock. The rain came down, the floods came, and the winds blew, and beat on that house; and it didn't fall, for it was founded on the rock. Everyone who hears these words of mine, and doesn't do them will be like a foolish man, who built his house on the sand. The rain came down, the floods came, and the winds blew, and beat on that house; and it fell--and great was its fall."
—[Matthew 7:24-27 and Luke 6:46-49 harmonized]**

It happened, when Jesus had finished saying these things, that the multitudes were astonished at His teaching, for He taught them with authority, and not like the scribes. —[Matthew 7:28-29]

CHAPTER 9

HEALING A CENTURION'S SERVANT

After Jesus had finished speaking to the people, He entered Capernaum. A certain centurion there had a servant who was dear to him, and the servant was sick and at the point of death. The servant lay in the house paralyzed and grievously tormented.

When the centurion heard about Jesus, he sent elders of the Jews to Him, asking Him to come and save his servant. The elders came to Jesus and earnestly begged Him, saying, "He is worthy for You to do this for him, for he loves our nation and built our synagogue for us."

Jesus replied saying *"I will come and heal him."* As He was not far from the house, the centurion sent friends to say to Him, "Lord, don't trouble Yourself, for I am not worthy for You to come under my roof. Therefore, I didn't even think myself worthy to come to You; but just say the word, and my servant will be healed. For I also am a man under authority, having soldiers under me. I tell this one, 'Go!' and he goes; and to another, 'Come!' and he comes; and to my servant, 'Do this,' and he does it."

When Jesus heard this, He marveled at the centurion and said to those who followed Him, *"Most assuredly I tell you, I have not found such great faith, not even in Israel. I tell you that many will come from the east and the west, and will sit down with Abraham, Isaac, and Jacob in the Kingdom of Heaven, but the children of the Kingdom will be thrown out into the outer darkness. There will be weeping and gnashing of teeth."*

Jesus then said to the centurion's friends, *"Go your way. Let it be done for you as you have believed."* Those who had been sent, returning to the house, found that the servant who had been sick was well, healed in that very hour. —[Matthew 8:5-13, Luke 7:1-10]

RAISING THE WIDOW'S SON AT NAIN

It happened soon afterwards that He went to a city called Nain. Many of
His disciples, along with a great multitude, went with Him. Now when He
drew near to the gate of the city, behold, one who was dead was carried
out, the only son of his mother, and she was a widow. Many people of the
city were with her. When the Lord saw her, He had compassion on her, and
said to her, *"Don't cry."* He came near and touched the coffin, and the
bearers stood still. He said, *"Young man, I tell you, arise!"* He who was
dead sat up, and began to speak. And He gave him to his mother.

Fear took hold of all, and they glorified God, saying, "A great prophet has
arisen among us!" and, "God has visited his people!" This report went out
concerning Him in the whole of Judea, and in all the surrounding region.
—[Luke 7:11-17]

MESSENGERS OF JOHN THE BAPTIST

After hearing about all these things, the disciples of John the Baptist came
to Him in prison and told Him about the works of Christ. Then, John sent
two of them to Jesus with the question, "Are You the one who is coming, or
should we look for another?"

When the men came to Jesus, they said, "John the Baptizer has sent us to
You, asking, 'Are You he who comes, or should we look for another?'"

At that time, Jesus was curing many people of diseases, plagues, and evil
spirits, and giving sight to many who were blind. Jesus answered them,
*"Go and tell John the things which you have seen and heard: the blind
receive their sight, the lame walk, the lepers are cleansed, the deaf
hear, the dead are raised up, and the poor have good news preached
to them. Blessed is he who is not offended by me."*

As John's disciples were leaving, Jesus began to speak to the crowds about
John: *"What did you go out into the wilderness to see? A reed shaken
by the wind? What then did you go out to see? A man clothed in soft
clothing? Behold, those who wear soft clothing and live delicately are*

in kings' houses. What then did you go out to see? A prophet? Yes, I tell you, and much more than a prophet. This is He of whom it is written,

'Behold, I send my messenger before Your face, who will prepare Your way before You.' Most assuredly, I tell you, among those who are born of women there has not arisen anyone greater than John the Baptizer; yet he who is least in the Kingdom of Heaven is greater than he."

When all the people and the tax collectors heard this, they declared God to be just, having been baptized with John's baptism. But the Pharisees and the lawyers rejected the counsel of God, not being baptized by him themselves.

Jesus continued, *"To what shall I liken the people of this generation? What are they like? They are like children sitting in the marketplace, who call to their companions and say, 'We played the flute for you, and you didn't dance. We mourned, and you didn't weep.' For John came neither eating bread nor drinking wine, and you say, 'He has a demon.' The Son of Man has come eating and drinking, and you say, 'Behold, a gluttonous man, and a drunkard; a friend of tax collectors and sinners!' But wisdom is justified by all her deeds (and by her children)."*

Jesus further explained, *"From the days of John the Baptizer until now, the Kingdom of Heaven suffers violence, and the violent take it by force. For all the prophets and the law prophesied until John. If you are willing to receive it, this is Elijah, who is to come. He who has ears to hear, let him hear."* —[Matthew 11:2-19, Luke 7:18-35]

It happened soon afterwards, that He went about through cities and villages, preaching and bringing the good news of the Kingdom of God. With Him were the twelve, and certain women who had been healed of evil spirits and infirmities: Mary who was called Magdalene, from whom seven demons had gone out; and Joanna, the wife of Chuzas, Herod's steward; Susanna; and many others; who ministered to them from their possessions.—[Luke 8:1-3]

Then a man who was possessed by a demon, blind and mute, was brought to Jesus and He healed him. It happened, when the demon had gone out, the man both spoke and saw. All the multitudes were amazed, and said, "Can this be the son of David?"—[Matthew 12:22-23]

JESUS & BEELZEBUB

But when the Pharisees heard this, they said, "This man casts out demons by Beelzebul, the prince of the demons." Others, scribes who had come down from Jerusalem were saying, "He is possessed by Beelzebul."

Knowing their thoughts, *Jesus called them to* Him and said to them in parables, *"How can Satan cast out Satan? If a kingdom is divided against itself, that kingdom cannot stand. And if a house is divided against itself, that house will not be able to stand either. And if Satan has risen up against himself and is divided, he cannot stand, but is coming to an end. But no one can enter a strong man's house and plunder his goods, unless he first binds the strong man. Then indeed he may plunder his house. Every kingdom divided against itself is brought to desolation, and every city or house divided against itself will not stand. If Satan casts out Satan, he is divided against himself. How then will his kingdom stand? If I by Beelzebul cast out demons, by whom do your children cast them out? Therefore they will be your judges. But if I by the Spirit of God cast out demons, then the Kingdom of God has come upon you. Or how can one enter into the house of the strong man, and plunder his goods, unless he first binds the strong man? Then he will plunder his house.*

"He who is not with me is against me, and he who doesn't gather with me, scatters. Therefore I tell you, every sin and blasphemy

will be forgiven men, but the blasphemy against the Holy Spirit will not be forgiven men. Whoever speaks a word against the Son of Man, it will be forgiven him; but whoever speaks against the Holy Spirit, it will not be forgiven him, neither in this age, nor in that which is to come." Jesus said this because they were saying, "He has an unclean spirit."

"Either make the tree good, and its fruit good, or make the tree corrupt, and its fruit corrupt; for the tree is known by its fruit. You offspring of vipers, how can you, being evil, speak good things? For out of the abundance of the heart, the mouth speaks. The good man out of his good treasure brings out good things, and the evil man out of his evil treasure brings out evil things. I tell you that every idle word that men speak, they will give account of it in the day of judgment. For by your words you will be justified, and by your words you will be condemned."*—[Matthew 12:24-37, Mark 3:22-30, and Luke 11:14-23]

Then certain of the scribes and Pharisees answered, "Teacher, we want to see a sign from you."

But he answered them, "An evil and adulterous generation seeks after a sign, but no sign will be given to it but the sign of Jonah the prophet. For as Jonah was three days and three nights in the belly of the huge fish, so will the Son of Man be three days and three nights in the heart of the earth. The men of Nineveh will stand up in the judgment with this generation and will condemn it, for they repented at the preaching of Jonah; and behold, someone greater than Jonah is here. The Queen of the South will rise up in the judgment with this generation and will condemn it, for she came from the ends of the earth to hear the wisdom of Solomon; and behold, someone greater than Solomon is here.

"When an unclean spirit has gone out of a man, he passes through waterless places seeking rest, and doesn't find it. Then he says, 'I will return into my house from which I came;' and when he has come back, he finds it empty, swept, and put in order. Then he goes and takes with himself seven other spirits more evil than he is, and they enter in and dwell there. The last state of that man becomes worse than the first. Even so will it be also to this evil generation." —[Matthew 12:37-45]

While He was yet speaking to the multitudes, behold, His mother and His brothers stood outside, seeking to speak to Him and take charge of Him; for they had heard of the multitude gathered around Him and intended to seize Him, for they had said "He is out of His mind!" *His family sent to Him and called Him. And a member of the crowd who was sitting around Him,* said to Him, "Your mother and Your brothers stand outside, seeking to speak to You."

But He answered him who spoke to Him, *"Who is my mother? Who are my brothers?"* He stretched out His hand towards His disciples, and said, *"Behold, my mother and my brothers! For whoever does the will of my Father who is in heaven, he is my brother, and sister, and mother."*—[Matthew 12:46-50; Mark 3:22-35; Luke 8:19-21 harmonized]

On that day Jesus went out of the house and sat by the seaside. [2] Great multitudes gathered to him, so that he entered into a boat and sat; and all the multitude stood on the beach as He began again to teach. [3] He spoke to them many things in parables, saying, "Behold, a farmer went out to sow. [4] As he sowed, some seeds fell by the roadside, and the birds came and devoured them. [5] Others fell on rocky ground, where they didn't have much soil, and immediately they sprang up, because they had no depth of earth. [6] When the sun had risen, they were scorched. Because they had no root, they withered away. [7] Others fell among thorns. The thorns grew up and choked them. [8] Others fell on good soil and yielded fruit: some one hundred times as much, some sixty, and some thirty. [9] He who has ears to hear, let him hear."

When He was alone, they who were around Him with the twelve came, and said to him, "Why do you speak to them in parables?"

[11] He answered them, "To you it is given to know the mysteries of the Kingdom of Heaven, but it is not given to them. [12] For whoever has, to him will be given, and he will have abundance; but whoever doesn't have, from him will be taken away even that which he has. [13] Therefore I speak to them in parables, because seeing they don't see, and hearing, they don't hear, neither do they understand. [14] In them the prophecy of Isaiah is fulfilled, which says,

'By hearing you will hear,
   and will in no way understand;
Seeing you will see,
   and will in no way perceive;

[15]

for this people's heart has grown callous,
   their ears are dull of hearing,
   and they have closed their eyes;
or else perhaps they might perceive with their eyes,
   hear with their ears,
   understand with their heart,
and would turn again,
   and I would heal them.'

[16] "But blessed are your eyes, for they see; and your ears, for they hear. [17] For most certainly I tell you that many prophets and righteous men desired to see the things which you see, and didn't see them; and to hear the things which you hear, and didn't hear them.

And He said to them. Do you not understand this parable? How will you understand all the parables?

"Listen then to what the parable of the sower means: The sower sows the word. When anyone hears the message about the kingdom and does not understand it, the evil one comes and snatches away what was sown in their heart. This is the seed sown along the path. The seed falling on rocky ground refers to someone who hears the word and at once receives it with joy. But since they have no root, they last only a

short time. When trouble or persecution comes because of the word, they quickly fall away. The seed falling among the thorns refers to someone who hears the word, but the worries of this life and the deceitfulness of wealth choke the word, making it unfruitful. But the seed falling on good soil refers to someone who hears the word, understands it, holding it fast in an honest and good heart, and bears fruit with patience. This same one produces a crop, yielding a hundred, sixty, or thirty times what was sown."

And He said to them, "Is a lamp brought to be put under a basket or under a bed? Isn't it to put on a stand? No one, when he has little lamp, covers it with a container, or puts it under a bed, but puts it on a stand, that those who enter in may see the light. For there is nothing hidden, except that it should be made known, neither was anything made secret, but that it should come to light. Be careful, therefore, how you hear. Take care what you listen to. By your standard of measure it will be measured to you; and more will be given beside. For whoever has, to him will be given, and whoever doesn't have, from him, even what he has or thinks he has will be taken away. If any man has ears to hear, let him hear."—[Matthew 13:1-23, Mark 4:1-25, and Luke 8:4-18]

PARABLES OF THE KINGDOM OF GOD:

**NOTE: Before you read, you may want to know what darnel is.
Typically known as **darnel, poison darnel, darnel ryegrass, cockle** or by taxonomy, *"Lolium temulentum,"*
darnel is an annual plant whose stem can grow up to one meter tall, with inflorescence in the ears and purple grain. It can be found almost anywhere in the world.**

He set another parable before them, saying, ***"The Kingdom of Heaven is like a man who sowed good seed in his field, but while people slept, his enemy came and sowed <u>darnel</u> also among the wheat, and went away. But when the blade sprang up and brought forth fruit, then the darnel appeared also. The servants of the householder came and said to him, 'Sir, didn't you sow good seed in your field? Where did this darnel come from?'***

"He said to them, 'An enemy has done this.'

"The servants asked him, 'Do you want us to go and gather them up?'

"But he said, 'No, lest perhaps while you gather up the darnel, you root up the wheat with them. Let both grow together until the harvest, and in the harvest time I will tell the reapers, "First, gather up the

darnel, and bind them in bundles to burn them; but gather the wheat into my barn."'

He set another parable before them, saying, *"The Kingdom of Heaven is like a grain of mustard seed, which a man took, and sowed in his field; which indeed is smaller than all seeds. But when it is grown, it is greater than the herbs, and becomes a tree, so that the birds of the air come and lodge in its branches and under its shadow."*

Jesus continued teaching His disciples using parables.

He said, "The Kingdom of God is as if a man should cast seed on the earth, and should sleep and rise night and day, and the seed should spring up and grow, he doesn't know how. For the earth bears fruit: first the blade, then the ear, then the full grain in the ear. But when the fruit is ripe, immediately he puts forth the sickle, because the harvest has come."

He spoke another parable to them. *"The Kingdom of Heaven is like yeast, which a woman took, and hid in three measures of meal, until it was all leavened."*

Jesus spoke all these things in parables to the multitudes; and without a parable, he didn't speak to them, that it might be fulfilled which was spoken through the prophet, saying,

"I will open my mouth in parables;
    I will utter things hidden from the foundation of the world."

Then Jesus sent the multitudes away, and went into the house. His disciples came to Him, saying, "Explain to us the parable of the darnel of the field."

He answered them, *"He who sows the good seed is the Son of Man, the field is the world; and the good seed, these are the children of the Kingdom; and the darnel are the children of the evil one. The enemy who sowed them is the devil. The harvest is the end of the age, and the reapers are angels. As therefore the darnel is gathered up and burned* with fire; so will it be at the end of this age. the Son of Man will send out His angels, and they will gather out of His Kingdom all things that cause stumbling, and those who do iniquity, and will cast them into the furnace of fire. There will be weeping and the gnashing of teeth. Then the righteous will shine forth like the sun in the Kingdom of their Father. He who has ears to hear, let him hear.

"Again, the Kingdom of Heaven is like a treasure hidden in the field, which a man found, and hid. In his joy, he goes and sells all that he has, and buys that field.

"Again, the Kingdom of Heaven is like a man who is a merchant seeking fine pearls, who having found one pearl of great price, he went and sold all that he had, and bought it.

"Again, the Kingdom of Heaven is like a dragnet, that was cast into the sea, and gathered some fish of every kind, which, when it was filled, they drew up on the beach. They sat down, and gathered the good into containers, but the bad they threw away. So will it be in the end of the world. The angels will come forth, and separate the wicked from among the righteous, and will cast them into the furnace of fire. There will be the weeping and the gnashing of teeth." Jesus said to them, "Have you understood all these things?"

They answered Him, "Yes, Lord."

He said to them, "Therefore, every scribe who has been made a disciple in the Kingdom of Heaven is like a man who is a householder, who brings out of his treasure new and old things."

[53] When Jesus had finished these parables, he departed from there. [54] Coming into his own country, he taught them in their synagogue, so that they were astonished and said, "Where did this man get this wisdom and these mighty works? [55] Isn't this the carpenter's son? Isn't his mother called Mary, and his brothers James, Joses, Simon, and Judas?[d] [56] Aren't all of his sisters with us? Where then did this man get all of these things?" [57] They were offended by him.

But Jesus said to them, "A prophet is not without honor, except in his own country and in his own house." [58] He didn't do many mighty works there because of their unbelief. —[Matthew 13:24-58, Mark 4:30-34, Luke 13:18-21]

THE COST OF DISCIPLESHIP

As they were going along the road, a scribe came and said to Him, "Teacher, I will follow You wherever You go."

Jesus said to him, *"The foxes have holes and the birds of the sky have nests, but the Son of Man has nowhere to lay His head."*

Another of His disciples said to Him, "Lord, allow me first to go and bury my father." But Jesus said to him, *"Follow me, and leave the dead to bury their own dead. But as for you, go and proclaim the Kingdom of God."* Yet another said, "I will follow You, Lord, but let me first say farewell to those at my home." Jesus replied to him, *"No one who puts his hand to the plow and looks back is fit for the Kingdom of God."*

Now when Jesus saw great multitudes around Him, He gave the order to depart to the other side.—[Matthew 8:18-22, Mark 3:7-12, and *Luke 9:57-62* harmonized]

JESUS CALMS A STORM

That evening, Jesus said to His disciples, "Let us go over to the other side of the lake." So they boarded a boat and set out, leaving the crowd behind. There were also other boats with them. As they sailed, Jesus was in the stern, sleeping on a cushion. Suddenly, a furious storm came and the waves began to break over the boat so that it was quickly collecting water. While the boat was being filled with water, the distressed disciples woke Him with their panicked cries. "Lord, save us! Teacher, Teacher! Don't you care if we drown? Master, Master! We're going to drown!!"

Jesus got up and rebuked the wind and the raging waters saying *"Quiet! Be still!"* Then the wind died down, and it was completely calm. Then, speaking to His disciples, He said, *"You of little faith, why are you so afraid? Where is your faith? Do you still have none?"* In fear and amazement, they asked each other, "Who is this? What kind of man is He? For even the wind and the waves obey Him!"—[Matthew 8:23-27, Mark 4:35-41, and Luke 8:22-25]

JESUS CASTS OUT LEGION

Jesus and His disciples came to the other side of the lake, in the region of the Gerasenes, Gergesenes, and Gardarenes (opposite Galilee). When He had stepped out on land, He saw two men who were demon possessed coming out of the tombs so fiercely and violently that no one could pass that way. They cried out, "What have you to do with us, O Son of God? Have You come here to torment us before the time? One of these men had lived naked among the tombs for a long time. The man, once restrainable, had become too strong to bind even with a chain, for he had often been bound with shackles and chains, but he wrenched the chains apart and broke the shackles in pieces and now, no one had the strength to subdue him. Night and day, he would cry incessantly while he cut himself with stones; and when he noticed Jesus from afar, he ran and fell down before Him. "What have you to do with me, Jesus, Son of the Most High God?" he cried." I adjure you by God, do not torment me!" For Jesus was telling the demons to come out of the men. Jesus asked the man who had fallen before Him, "What is your name?" He replied, "My name is Legion, for we are many." And he begged Jesus earnestly not to send them out of the country. Now a large herd of pigs was feeding on a hillside nearby, and they begged Jesus, saying, "Send us to the pigs; let us enter them." So He gave them permission. At once, the unclean spirits came out of the men and entered the pigs; and the herd, numbering about two thousand rushed down the steep bank into the sea where they drowned.

Those who fed them fled, and told it in the city and in the country. The people came to see what had happened. They came to Jesus, and saw him who had been possessed by demons sitting, clothed, and in his right mind, even him who had the legion; and they were afraid. Those who saw it declared to them how it happened to him who was possessed by demons, and about the pigs. Then, the people began to beg Jesus to depart from their region.

As Jesus was entering into the boat, he who had been possessed by demons begged Him that he might be with Him. Jesus didn't allow him, but said to him, "Go to your house, to your friends, and tell them what great things the Lord has done for you, and how He had mercy on you." He went his way, and began to proclaim in Decapolis how Jesus had done great things for him, and everyone marveled. —[Matthew 8:28-34, Mark 5:1-20, and Luke 8:26-39]

CHAPTER 10

HEALING THE WOMAN WITH THE ISSUE OF BLOOD & JAIRUS' DAUGHTER

When Jesus had crossed back over in the boat to the other side, a great multitude was gathered to Him; and He was by the sea. Behold, one of the rulers of the synagogue, Jairus by name, came; and seeing Him, he fell at His feet, and begged Him much, saying, "My little daughter is at the point of death. Please come and lay Your hands on her, that she may be made healthy, and live."

He went with him, and a great multitude followed Him, and they pressed upon Him on all sides. A certain woman, who had an issue of blood for twelve years, had suffered many things by many physicians, and had spent all that she had, and was no better, but rather grew worse, for no one had been able to heal her. Having heard the things concerning Jesus, she came up behind him in the crowd, and touched his clothes. For she said, "If I just touch his clothes, I will be made well." Immediately the flow of her blood was dried up, and she felt in her body that she was healed of her affliction.

Instantly, Jesus, perceiving in himself that the power had gone out from Him, turned around in the crowd, and asked, "Who touched my clothes?"

His disciples said to Him, "You see the multitude pressing against You, and You say, 'Who touched me?'"

He looked around to see her who had done this thing. But the woman, fearing and trembling, knowing what had been done to her, and that she was not hidden came trembling and fell down before Him. Declaring the whole truth in the presence of all the people, she made known why she had touched Him and how she had been healed that very moment.

He said to her, ***"Daughter, your faith has made you well. Go in peace, and be cured of your disease."***

While He was still speaking, someone came from the synagogue ruler's house saying, "Your daughter is dead. Why bother the Teacher any more?"

But Jesus, when He heard the message spoken, immediately said to Jairus, *"Don't be afraid, only believe and she will be well."* When He came to the house, Jesus allowed no one to follow him, except Peter, James, John the brother of James, and the father and mother of the child. Entering in, He saw flute players and the crowd making a commotion with weeping, and great wailing and asked them, *"Why do you make an uproar and weep? The child is not dead, but is asleep."*

They laughed at and ridiculed Him. But Jesus, putting them all out, took the father of the child and her mother and those who were with Him, and went in where the child was lying. He took the child by the hand and said to her, *"Talitha cumi;"* which means, being interpreted, *"Girl, I tell you, get up."* Immediately the girl rose up, and walked. She was twelve years old. They were amazed with great amazement. He strictly ordered them that no one should know this, and commanded that something should be given to her to eat. Nevertheless, the report went through all that district. —[Matthew 9:18-26, Mark 5:21-43, and Luke 8:40-56 harmonized]

JESUS HEALS TWO BLIND MEN & ONE WHO WAS MUTE

As Jesus passed by from there, two blind men followed Him, calling out and saying, "Have mercy on us, son of David!" When He had come into the house, the blind men came to Him. Jesus said to them, *"Do you believe that I am able to do this?"* They told Him, "Yes, Lord."Then He touched their eyes, saying, *"According to your faith be it done to you."* Their eyes were opened. Jesus strictly charged them, saying, *"See that no one knows about this."* But they went out and spread abroad His fame in all that land. As they went out, behold, a mute man who was demon possessed was brought to Him. When the demon was cast out, the mute man spoke. The multitudes marveled, saying, "Nothing like this has ever been seen in Israel!" But the Pharisees said, "By the prince of the demons, He casts out demons."—[Matthew 9:27-34]

REJECTED AT NAZARETH [...AGAIN?]

Jesus went out from there and and His disciples followed Him. He returned to His hometown and when the Sabbath came, He taught them in the synagogue, so they and many listeners were astonished, saying, "Where did this man get such wisdom and miraculous power? Isn't this Joseph the carpenter's son and a carpenter also? Isn't his mother Mary? And aren't his brothers James, Joseph, Simon, and Judas? Aren't his sisters with us? Where then did he get all these things?" And they were offended by him. Jesus said to them, "A prophet is not without honor except in his hometown and in his own household. And he did not do many mighty works there, except that He laid His hands on a few sick people and healed them, because of their unbelief.—[Matthew 13:53-58, Mark 6:1-6]

DEATH of JOHN the BAPTIST

Meanwhile, on Herod's birthday, he gave a banquet for his high officials, military commanders, and the leading men of Galilee. The daughter of Herodias came in and danced, pleasing Herod and his dinner guests. The king, impressed with the girl, said to her, "Ask me for anything you want, and I will give it to you." He promised this with an oath that whatever she would ask of him, he would give her up to half his kingdom.

Now Herod had already arrested and imprisoned John on account of Herodias, his brother Philip's wife, whom Herod had married. John had said to him, "It is not lawful for you to have her." Herodias who, in response, had begun to nurse a grudge against John, wanted to kill him for this reason, but she was unable to because Herod feared John and protected him, knowing him to be a righteous and holy man. Moreover, the multitude that followed him would likely riot. King Herod's relationship with John was further complicated by the fact that whenever Herod would hear John speak, he was greatly puzzled, yet he enjoyed listening to him.

Prompted by her mother that evening, Herodias' daughter said, "Give me, here on a platter, the head of John the Baptist." The king was greatly distressed, but because of his oaths and his dinner guests, he did not want to refuse her. So he immediately sent an executioner with orders to bring

John's head. The man went, beheaded John in the prison, and brought back his head on a platter. He presented it to the girl, and she gave it to her mother.

Then, John's disciples came, took his body, laid it in a tomb. and went to tell Jesus.—Matthew 14:1-12, Mark 6:14-29, *and referenced by* Luke 9:7-9]

Jesus was going through all the cities and villages, teaching in their synagogues and proclaiming the gospel of the kingdom, and healing every disease and every sickness. Seeing the crowds, he felt compassion for them, because they were distressed and downcast, like sheep without a shepherd. Then he said to his disciples,

"The harvest is plentiful, but the laborers are few. Therefore pray earnestly to the Lord of the harvest to send out laborers into His harvest. —[Matthew 9:35-38]

SENDING OUT THE 12 APOSTLES

Jesus called His twelve disciples together and gave them power and authority to drive out impure spirits and to heal every disease and sickness. He began to send them out two by two to proclaim the kingdom of God and to heal the sick.

These are the names of the twelve apostles: Simon (who is called Peter) and his brother Andrew; James son of Zebedee and his brother John; Philip and Bartholomew; Thomas and Matthew the tax collector; James son of Alphaeus and Thaddaeus (a.k.a Jude and also less commonly, Judas); Simon the Zealot and Judas Iscariot, who betrayed him.

Jesus gave them the following instructions: *"Do not go among the Gentiles or enter any town of the Samaritans. Go rather to the lost sheep of Israel. As you go, proclaim this message: 'The kingdom of heaven has come near.' Heal the sick, raise the dead, cleanse those who have leprosy, drive out demons. Freely you have received; freely give."*

"Take nothing for the journey—no staff, no bag, no bread, no money, no extra shirt. Wear sandals, but not an extra shirt. For the worker is worth his keep."

"Whatever town or village you enter, search there for some worthy person and stay at their house until you leave. As you enter the home, give it your greeting. If the home is deserving, let your peace rest on it; if it is not, let your peace return to you. If anyone will not welcome you or listen to your words, leave that home or town and shake the dust off your feet as a testimony against them. "Truly I tell you, it will be more bearable for Sodom and Gomorrah on the day of judgment than for that town. I am sending you out like sheep among wolves. Therefore be as shrewd as snakes and as innocent as doves. Be on your guard; you will be handed over to the local councils and be flogged in the synagogues. On my account you will be brought before governors and kings as witnesses to them and to the Gentiles. But when they arrest you, do not worry about what to say or how to say it. At that time you will be given what to say, for it will not be you speaking, but the Spirit of your Father speaking through you. Brother will betray brother to death, and a father his child; children will rebel against their parents and have them put to death. You will be hated by everyone because of me, but the one who stands firm to the end will be saved. When you are persecuted in one place, flee to another. Truly I tell you, you will not finish going through the towns of Israel before the Son of Man comes."

"The student is not above the teacher, nor a servant above his master. It is enough for students to be like their teachers, and servants like their masters. If the head of the house has been called Beelzebul, how much more the members of his household!"

"So do not be afraid of them, for there is nothing concealed that will not be disclosed, or hidden that will not be made known. What I tell you in the dark, speak in the daylight; what is whispered in your ear, proclaim from the roofs. Do not be afraid of those who kill the body

but cannot kill the soul. Rather, be afraid of the One who can destroy both soul and body in hell. Are not two sparrows sold for a penny? Yet not one of them will fall to the ground outside your Father's care. And even the very hairs of your head are all numbered. So don't be afraid; you are worth more than many sparrows."

"Whoever acknowledges me before others, I will also acknowledge before my Father in heaven. But whoever disowns me before others, I will disown before my Father in heaven. Do not suppose that I have come to bring peace to the earth. I did not come to bring peace, but a sword. For I have come to turn 'a man against his father, a daughter against her mother, a daughter-in-law against her mother-in-law— a man's enemies will be the members of his own household.' Anyone who loves their father or mother more than me is not worthy of me; anyone who loves their son or daughter more than me is not worthy of me. Whoever does not take up their cross and follow me is not worthy of me. Whoever finds their life will lose it, and whoever loses their life for my sake will find it."

"Anyone who welcomes you welcomes me, and anyone who welcomes me welcomes the one who sent me. Whoever welcomes a prophet as a prophet will receive a prophet's reward, and whoever welcomes a righteous person as a righteous person will receive a righteous person's reward. And if anyone gives even a cup of cold water to one of these little ones who is my disciple, truly I tell you, that person will certainly not lose their reward."—[Matthew 10:15-42]

When Jesus had finished instructing the twelve, He went on from there to teach and preach in their cities. They also went out in pairs and preached the gospel and that men should repent. And they were casting out many demons and were anointing with oil many sick people and healing them.—[Matthew 10-11:1, Mark 6:7-13, and Luke 9:1-6]

And King Herod the tetrarch heard of all that was happening, for His name had become well known; and people were saying, "John the Baptist has risen from the dead, and that is why these miraculous powers are at work in Him." But others were saying, "He is Elijah." And others were saying, "He is a prophet, like one of the prophets of old." But when Herod heard of it, he was greatly perplexed and he kept saying, "John, whom I beheaded, has risen! I myself had John beheaded; but who is this man about whom I hear such things?" And he kept trying to see Him.—[Mark 6:14-16, Luke 9:7-9]

Luke 9 & 10...the 72...then the 72 return...

Then He began to denounce the cities in which most of His mighty works had been done, because they didn't repent. *"Woe to you, Chorazin! Woe to you, Bethsaida! For if the mighty works had been done in Tyre and Sidon which were done in you, they would have repented long ago in sackcloth and ashes. But I tell you, it will be more tolerable for Tyre and Sidon on the day of judgment than for you. You, Capernaum, who are exalted to Heaven, you will go down to Hades. For if the mighty works had been done in Sodom which were done in you, it would have remained until this day. But I tell you that it will be more tolerable for the land of Sodom, on the day of judgment, than for you."*—[Matthew 11:20-24]

"Come to me, all you who labor and are heavily burdened, and I will give you rest. Take my yoke upon you, and learn from me, for I am gentle and lowly in heart; and you will find rest for your souls. For my yoke is easy, and my burden is light."—[Matthew 11:28-30]

CHAPTER 11

FEEDING FIVE THOUSAND

When Jesus heard of the death of John the Baptist, He withdrew with His disciples in a boat to a deserted place. So they went away by themselves in a boat to a solitary place. But many who saw them leaving recognized them, others heard the news, and they ran on foot from all the towns and got there ahead of them. When Jesus landed and saw a large crowd, He had compassion on them, because they were like sheep without a shepherd. So He began teaching them many things and spoke to them about the kingdom of God, and healed those who needed healing.

When Jesus looked up and saw a great crowd coming toward Him, He said to Philip, "Where shall we buy bread for these people to eat?" He asked this only to test Him, for He already had in mind what He was going to do. Philip answered Him, "It would take more than half a year's wages to buy enough bread for each one to have a bite!" Another of His disciples, Andrew (Simon Peter's brother) spoke up, "Here is a boy with five small barley loaves and two small fish, but how far will they go among so many?"

As evening approached, the disciples came to Him and said, "This is a remote place, and it's already getting late. Send the crowds away so they can go to the villages and buy themselves some food."

But Jesus replied, *"They do not need to go away. You give them something to eat."*

They said to Him, "That would take more than half a year's wages! Are we to go and spend that much on bread and give it to them to eat? We have only five loaves of bread and two fish—unless we go and buy food for all this crowd."

About five thousand men were there, besides women and children. But Jesus said to His disciples, *"Have them sit down in groups of about fifty each."* The disciples did so, and everyone sat down. Jesus then took the five loaves and the two fish, looked up to heaven, and gave thanks. He broke the loaves, then gave them to the disciples to distribute to the people. He did the same with the fish. They all ate and were satisfied.

When they all had eaten enough, Jesus said to His disciples, *"Gather the pieces that are left over. Let nothing be wasted."* So they gathered them and filled twelve baskets with the pieces of the five barley loaves left over by those who had eaten. And they who had eaten were about five thousand men

Immediately after feeding the crowd, Jesus made His disciples get into the boat and go on ahead of Him toward the region of Bethsaida and Capernaum, while He dismissed the crowd. After the people saw the sign Jesus performed, they began to say, "Surely this is the Prophet who is to come into the world." Jesus, knowing that they intended to come and make Him king by force, withdrew again to a mountain to pray by Himself. —[Matthew 14:13-21, Mark 6:30-44, and Luke 9:10-17, and John 6:1-15]

WALKING ON WATER

When evening came, the boat was in the middle of the lake, and Jesus was alone on land. It was dark, and He had not yet joined His disciples. A strong wind was blowing, and the waters grew rough. The disciples were straining at the oars because the wind was against them. Shortly before dawn, (after He had finished praying), Jesus went out to them, walking on the lake. He was about to pass by them, but when they saw Him walking on the lake, they were terrified. "It's a ghost," they cried out.

Immediately Jesus spoke to them and said, *"Take courage! I AM... Don't be afraid."*

"Lord, if it's you," Peter replied, "tell me to come to you on the water."

"Come," He said.

Then Peter got down out of the boat, walked on the water, and came toward Jesus. But when he saw the wind, he was afraid and, beginning to sink, he cried out, "Lord, save me!"

Immediately Jesus reached out His hand and caught him. *"You of little faith,"* He said, *"why did you doubt?"*

When they climbed into the boat, the wind died down. They were completely amazed, for they had not understood about the loaves; for their hearts were hardened. Then those who were in the boat worshiped Him, saying, "Truly you are the Son of God."

Immediately the boat reached the shore in the direction they were heading. —[Matthew 14:22-33, Mark 6:45-52, and John 6:16-21 harmonized]

HEALING IN GENNESARET

When Jesus and His disciples had crossed over the lake, they landed and anchored at Gennesaret. As soon as they got out of the boat, the people recognized Him. The men of that place sent word to all the surrounding country, and people ran throughout the whole region. They brought all their sick on mats to wherever they heard Jesus was.

Wherever He went—into villages, towns, or the countryside—people placed the sick in the marketplaces. They begged Him to let the sick just touch the edge of His cloak, and all who touched it were healed. —[Matthew 14:34-36 and Mark 6:53-56]

WHO DO THEY SAY I AM?

Once when Jesus was praying in private with His disciples, He asked them, *"Who do the crowds say I am?"*

They replied, "Some say John the Baptist; others say Elijah; and still others, Jeremiah or one of the prophets of long ago has come back to life."

"But what about you?" He asked. *"Who do you say I am?"*

Simon Peter answered, "You are the Messiah, the Son of the living God."

Jesus replied, *"Blessed are you, Simon son of Jonah, for this was not revealed to you by flesh and blood, but by my Father in heaven. And I tell you that you are Peter, and on this rock I will build my church, and the gates of Hades will not overcome it. I will give you the keys of the kingdom of heaven; whatever you bind on earth will be bound in heaven, and whatever you loose on earth will be loosed in heaven."*

Jesus then warned His disciples not to tell anyone that He was the Messiah. This occurred when Jesus was in the region of Caesarea Philippi.—[Matthew 16:13-20, Mark 8:27-30, and Luke 9:18-20]

FALLING AWAY

On the next day, the multitude that stood on the other side of the sea saw that there was no other boat there, except the one in which His disciples had embarked, and that Jesus hadn't entered with His disciples into the boat, but His disciples had gone away alone. However boats from Tiberias came near to the place where they ate the bread after the Lord had given thanks. When the multitude therefore saw that Jesus wasn't there, nor His disciples, they themselves got into the boats, and came to Capernaum, seeking Jesus. When they found Him on the other side of the sea, they asked him, "Rabbi, when did you come here?"

Jesus answered them, *"Most assuredly I tell you, you seek me, not because you saw signs, but because you ate of the loaves, and were filled. Don't work for the food which perishes, but for the food which remains to eternal life, which the Son of Man will give to you. For God the Father has sealed Him."*

They said therefore to Him, "What must we do, that we may work the works of God?"

Jesus answered them, *"This is the work of God, that you believe in Him whom He has sent."*

They said therefore to Him, "What then do You do for a sign, that we may see, and believe You? What work do You do? Our fathers ate the manna in the wilderness. As it is written, 'He gave them bread out of heaven to eat.'"

Jesus therefore said to them, *"Most assuredly, I tell you, it wasn't Moses who gave you the bread out of heaven, but my Father gives you the true bread out of heaven. For the bread of God is that which comes down out of heaven, and gives life to the world."*

They said therefore to Him, "Lord, always give us this bread."

Jesus said to them, *"I am the bread of life. He who comes to me will not be hungry, and he who believes in me will never be thirsty. But I told you that you have seen me, and yet you don't believe. All those who the Father gives me will come to me. Him who comes to me I will in no way throw out. For I have come down from heaven, not to do my own will, but the will of Him who sent me. This is the will of the one who sent me; my Father, that of all he has given to me I should lose nothing, but should raise him up at the last day and that everyone who sees the Son, and believes in Him, should have eternal life; for I will raise him up at the last day."*

The Jews therefore murmured concerning Him, because He said, *"I am the bread which came down out of heaven."* They said, "Isn't this Jesus, the son of Joseph, whose father and mother we know? How then does He say, *'I have come down out of heaven?'"*

Therefore Jesus answered them, *"Don't murmur among yourselves. No one can come to me unless the Father who sent me draws him. It is written in the prophets, 'They will all be taught by God.' Therefore everyone who hears from the Father, and has learned, comes to me. Not that anyone has seen the Father, except He who is from God. He has seen the Father. Most assuredly, I tell you, he who believes in me has eternal life. For I am the bread of life. Your fathers ate the manna in the wilderness, and they died. This, however, is the bread which comes down out of heaven, that anyone may eat of it and not die. I am that living bread which came down out of heaven. If anyone eats of this bread, he will live forever. Yes, the bread which I will give for the life of the world is my flesh."*

The Jews therefore contended with one another, saying, "How can this man give us His flesh to eat?"

Jesus therefore said to them, *"Most assuredly I tell you, unless you eat the flesh of the Son of Man and drink His blood, you don't have life in yourselves. He who eats my flesh and drinks my blood has eternal life, and I will raise him up at the last day. For my flesh is food indeed, and my blood is drink indeed. He who eats my flesh and drinks my blood lives in me, and I in him. As the living Father sent me, and I live because of the Father; so he who feeds on me, he will also live because of me. This is the bread which came down out of heaven-- not as our fathers ate the manna, and died. He who eats this bread will live forever."* These things He said in the synagogue, as He taught in Capernaum.

Therefore many of His disciples, when they heard this, said, "This is a hard saying! Who can listen to it?"

But Jesus knowing in Himself that His disciples murmured at this, said to them, *"Does this cause you to stumble? Then what if you would see the Son of Man ascending to where He was before? It is the spirit who gives life. The flesh profits nothing. The words that I speak to you are spirit, and are life. But there are some of you who don't believe."* For Jesus knew from the beginning who they were who didn't believe, and who it was who would betray Him. He said, *"For this cause have I said to you that no one can come to me, unless it is given to him by my Father."*

At this, many of His disciples went back, and walked no more with Him. Jesus said therefore to the twelve, *"You don't also want to go away, do you?"*

Simon Peter answered Him, "Lord, to whom would we go? You have the words of eternal life. We have come to believe and know that You are the Christ, the Son of the living God."

Jesus answered them, *"Didn't I choose you, the twelve, and one of you is a devil?"* Now He spoke of Judas, the son of Simon Iscariot, for it was he who would betray Him, being one of the twelve. —[John 6:22-71]

WHAT TRULY DEFILES SOMEONE

Then some Pharisees and teachers of the law who had come from Jerusalem gathered around Jesus and saw some of His disciples eating food with hands that were defiled, that is, unwashed. The Pharisees and all the Jews do not eat unless they give their hands a ceremonial washing, holding to the tradition of the elders. When they come from the marketplace they do not eat unless they wash. And they observe many other traditions, such as the washing of cups, pitchers, and kettles.

The Pharisees and teachers of the law asked Jesus, "Why do Your disciples break the tradition of the elders? They don't wash their hands before they eat!"

Jesus replied, *"And why do you break the command of God for the sake of your tradition? For God said, 'Honor your father and mother' and 'Anyone who curses their father or mother is to be put to death.' But you say that if anyone declares that what might have been used to help their father or mother is 'Corban' (that is, devoted to God), they are not to 'honor their father or mother' with it. Thus you nullify the word of God for the sake of your tradition that you have handed down. And you do many things like that. You hypocrites! Isaiah was right when he prophesied about you: 'These people honor me with their lips, but their hearts are far from me. They worship me in vain; their teachings are merely human rules.' You have let go of the commands of God and are holding on to human traditions."*

Jesus called the crowd to Him and said, *"Listen and understand. What goes into someone's mouth does not defile them, but what comes out of their mouth, that is what defiles them."*

Then the disciples came to Him and asked, *"Do you know that the Pharisees were offended when they heard this?"*

He replied, *"Every plant that my heavenly Father has not planted will be pulled up by the roots. Leave them; they are blind guides. If the blind lead the blind, both will fall into a pit."*

After He had left the crowd and entered the house, His disciples asked Him about this parable. Peter said, "Explain the parable to us."

"Are you still so dull?" Jesus asked them. *"Don't you see that whatever enters the mouth goes into the stomach and then out of the body? For it doesn't go into their heart but into their stomach, and then out of the body."* (In saying this, Jesus declared all foods clean.) He went on: *"But the things that come out of a person's mouth come from the heart, and these defile them. For out of the heart come evil thoughts—sexual immorality, theft, murder, adultery, greed, malice, deceit, lewdness, envy, slander, arrogance, and folly. These are what defile a person; but eating with unwashed hands does not defile them."*—[Matthew 15:1-20 and Mark 7:1-23 *harmonized*]

THE SYROPHOENICIAN WOMAN'S DAUGHTER

Leaving that place, Jesus withdrew to the region of Tyre and Sidon. He entered a house and did not want anyone to know it, yet He could not keep His presence secret. A Canaanite woman (a Greek, born in Syrian Phoenicia) from that vicinity came to Him as soon as she heard about Him. She cried out, "Lord, Son of David, have mercy on me! My daughter is demon-possessed and suffering terribly."

Jesus did not answer a word. So His disciples came to Him and urged Him, "Send her away, for she keeps crying out after us." He answered, *"I was sent only to the lost sheep of Israel."*

The woman came and knelt before Him. "Lord, help me!" she said. Jesus replied, *"It is not right to take the children's bread and toss it to the dogs."*

"Yes it is, Lord," she said. "Even the dogs eat the crumbs that fall from their master's table."

Then Jesus said to her, *"Woman, you have great faith! For such a reply, you may go; the demon has left your daughter."* Her request was granted. She went home and found her child lying on the bed, and the demon gone. —[Matthew 15:21-28, Mark 7:24-30]

CHAPTER 12

HEALING A DEAF, AND MUTE MAN

Again He departed from the borders of Tyre and Sidon, and came to the sea of Galilee, through the midst of the region of Decapolis. They brought to Him one who was deaf and had an impediment in his speech. They begged Him to lay his hand on him. He took him aside from the multitude, privately, and put His fingers into his ears, and He spat, and touched his tongue. Looking up to heaven, He sighed, and said to him, *"Ephphatha!"* that is, *"Be opened!"* Immediately his ears were opened, and the impediment of his tongue was released, and he spoke clearly. Jesus commanded them that they should tell no one, but the more He commanded them, so much the more widely they proclaimed it. They were astonished beyond measure, saying, "He has done all things well. He makes even the deaf hear, and the mute speak!"—[Mark 7:31-37]

FEEDING ANOTHER MULTITUDE

Jesus departed there, and came near to the sea of Galilee; and He went up into the mountain, and sat there. Great multitudes came to Him, having with them the lame, blind, mute, maimed, and many others, and they put them down at His feet. He healed them, so that the multitude wondered when they saw the mute speaking, injured whole, lame walking, and blind seeing--and they glorified the God of Israel. They had nothing to eat, so Jesus called His disciples to Himself, and said to them, *"I have compassion on the multitude, because they have stayed with me now three days, and have nothing to eat. If I send them away fasting to their home, they will faint on the way, for some of them have come a long way."*

The disciples said to Him, "Where should we get so many loaves in a deserted place as to satisfy so great a multitude?"

Jesus said to them, *"How many loaves do you have?"*

They said, "Seven, and a few small fish."

He commanded the multitude to sit down on the ground; and He took the seven loaves and the fish. He gave thanks and broke them, and gave to the disciples, and the disciples to the multitudes. They all ate, and were filled. They took up seven baskets full of the broken pieces that were left over. Those who ate were four thousand men, besides women and children. Then He sent away the multitudes, got into the boat, and came into the borders of Magdala in the region of Dalmanutha. —[Matthew 15:29-39 and Mark 8:1-10]

THE LEAVEN OF THE PHARISEES AND SADDUCEES (& THE SIGN OF JONAH)

The Pharisees and Sadducees came, and testing Him, asked Him to show them a sign from heaven. But He answered them, *"When it is evening, you say, 'It will be fair weather, for the sky is red.' In the morning, 'It will be foul weather today, for the sky is red and threatening.' Hypocrites! You know how to discern the appearance of the sky, but you can't discern the signs of the times!*

An evil and adulterous generation seeks after a sign, and there will be no sign given to it, except the sign of the prophet Jonah."

Entering a boat with His disciples, He left them. He and the disciples came to the other side and had forgotten to take bread. Jesus said to them, *"Take heed and beware of the yeast of the Pharisees and Sadducees."* They reasoned among themselves, saying, "We brought no bread."

Jesus, perceiving it, said, *"Why do you reason among yourselves, you of little faith, 'because you have brought no bread?' Don't you yet perceive, neither remember the five loaves for the five thousand, and how many baskets you took up? Nor the seven loaves for the four thousand, and how many baskets you took up? How is it that you don't perceive that I didn't speak to you concerning bread? But beware of the yeast of the Pharisees and Sadducees."*

Then they understood that He didn't tell them to beware of the yeast of bread, but of the teaching of the Pharisees and Sadducees. —[Matthew 16:1-12 and Mark 8:11-21]

HEALING A BLIND MAN AT BETHSAIDA

He came to Bethsaida. They brought a blind man to Him, and begged Him to touch him. He took hold of the blind man by the hand, and brought him out of the village. When He had spit on his eyes, and laid His hands on him, He asked him if he saw anything.

He looked up, and said, "I see men; for I see them like trees walking."

Then again He laid His hands on his eyes. He looked intently, and was restored, and saw everyone clearly. He sent him away to his house, saying, *"Don't enter into the village, nor tell anyone in the village."*—[Mark 8:22-26]

JESUS FORETELLS HIS DEATH (The First Time)

From that time on, Jesus began to explain to His disciples that He must go to Jerusalem and suffer many things at the hands of the elders, the chief priests, and the teachers of the law, and that He must be killed and on the third day be raised to life. He spoke plainly about this.

Peter took Him aside and began to rebuke Him. "Never, Lord!" he said. "This shall never happen to You!"

But Jesus turned and looked at His disciples, rebuked Peter, and said, *"Get behind me, Satan! You are a stumbling block to me; you do not have in mind the concerns of God, but merely human concerns."*

Then He called the crowd to Himself along with His disciples and said: *"Whoever wants to be my disciple must deny themselves and take up their cross daily and follow me. For whoever wants to save their life will lose it, but whoever loses their life for me and for the gospel will save it. What good is it for someone to gain the whole world, yet forfeit their soul? Or what can anyone give in exchange for their soul? If anyone is ashamed of me and my words, the Son of Man will be ashamed of them when He comes in His Father's glory with the holy angels. Truly I tell you, some who are standing here will not taste death before they see the Son of Man coming in His kingdom—that is, the kingdom of God.*"—[Matthew 16:21-28, Mark 8:31-9:1, and Luke 9:21-27]

CHAPTER 13

TRANSFIGURED

After six days, Jesus took with Him Peter, James, and John the brother of James, and led them up a high mountain by themselves to pray. As He was praying, His face changed, and His clothes became as bright as a flash of lightning, dazzling white, whiter than anyone in the world could bleach them.

There He was transfigured before them. His face shone like the sun, and His clothes became as white as the light. And there appeared before them Elijah and Moses, who were talking with Jesus. They spoke about His departure, which He was about to bring to fulfillment at Jerusalem.

Peter and his companions were very sleepy, but when they became fully awake, they saw His glory and the two men standing with Him. As the men were leaving Jesus, Peter said to Him, "Rabbi, it is good for us to be here. Let us put up three shelters—one for You, one for Moses, and one for Elijah." (He did not know what he was saying.)

While He was still speaking, a bright cloud covered them, and a voice from the cloud said, "This is my Son, whom I love; with Him I am well pleased. Listen to Him!"

When the disciples heard this, they fell facedown to the ground, terrified. But Jesus came and touched them. "Get up," He said. ***"Don't be afraid."*** When they looked up, they saw no one except Jesus.

As they were coming down the mountain, Jesus instructed them, ***"Don't tell anyone what you have seen, until the Son of Man has been raised from the dead."*** The disciples kept this to themselves, and did not tell anyone at that time what they had seen.

The disciples asked Him, "Why then do the teachers of the law say that Elijah must come first?"

Jesus replied, ***"To be sure, Elijah does come first, and restores all things. Why then is it written that the Son of Man must suffer much*** *and be rejected? But I tell you, Elijah has already come, and they did not recognize him, but have done to him everything they wished. In the same way, the Son of Man is going to suffer at their hands."* Then the disciples understood that when He had said, *"Elijah has already come, and they did not recognize him,"* He was talking to them about John the Baptist. —[Matthew 17:1-13, Mark 9:2-13, and Luke 9:28-36]

HEALING A BOY WITH A DEMON

The next day, when they came down from the mountain to join the other disciples, they saw a large crowd around them, and the teachers of the law arguing with them. As soon as all the people saw Jesus, they were overwhelmed with wonder and ran to greet Him.

A man in the crowd approached Jesus and knelt before Him. "Teacher, I brought you my son, who is possessed by a spirit that has robbed him of speech. Whenever it seizes him, it throws him to the ground. He foams at the mouth, gnashes his teeth, and becomes rigid. I asked your disciples to drive out the spirit, but they could not."

"You unbelieving and perverse generation," Jesus replied, *"how long shall I stay with you? How long shall I put up with you? Bring the boy here to me."*

So they brought him. When the spirit saw Jesus, it immediately threw the boy into a convulsion. He fell to the ground and rolled around, foaming at the mouth. Jesus asked the boy's father, *"How long has he been like this?"*

"From childhood," he answered. "It has often thrown him into fire or water to kill him. But if you can do anything, take pity on us and help us."

"'If you can'?" said Jesus. *"Everything is possible for one who believes."*

Immediately the boy's father exclaimed, "I do believe; help me overcome my unbelief!"

When Jesus saw that a crowd was running to the scene, He rebuked the impure spirit. *"You deaf and mute spirit,"* He said, *"I command you, come out of him and never enter him again."*

The spirit shrieked, convulsed him violently, and came out. The boy looked so much like a corpse that many said, "He's dead." But Jesus took him by the hand and lifted him to his feet, and he stood up. And the boy was healed from that moment.

They were all amazed at the greatness of God. After Jesus had gone indoors, His disciples asked Him privately, "Why couldn't we drive it out?"

He replied, *"Because you have so little faith. Truly I tell you, if you have faith as small as a mustard seed, you can say to this mountain, 'Move from here to there,' and it will move. Nothing will be impossible for you. This kind can come out only by prayer and fasting."*—[Matthew 17:14-21, Mark 9:14-29, Luke 9:37-43 *harmonized*]

CHAPTER 14

JESUS PREDICTS HIS DEATH AGAIN

While everyone was marveling at all that Jesus did, He said to His disciples, *"Listen carefully to what I am about to tell you: The Son of Man is going to be betrayed and delivered into the hands of men. They will kill Him, and after three days He will rise."* They were exceedingly sorry. But they did not really understand what this meant. It was hidden from them, so that they did not grasp it, and they were afraid to ask Him about it. —[Matthew 17:22-23, Mark 9:30, Luke 9:43-45]

THE TEMPLE TAX

When they had come to Capernaum, those who collected the didrachma coins came to Peter, and said, "Doesn't your teacher pay the didrachma?" He said, "Yes."

When he came into the house, Jesus anticipated him, saying, *"What do you think, Simon? From whom do the kings of the earth receive toll or tribute? From their children, or from strangers?"*

Peter said to Him, "From strangers."

Jesus said to him, *"Therefore the children are exempt. But, lest we cause them to stumble, go to the sea, and cast a hook, and take up the first fish that comes up. When you have opened its mouth, you will find a stater coin. Take that, and give it to them for me and you."*—[Matthew 17:24-27]

WHO IS THE GREATEST?

At that time the disciples came to Jesus and asked, "Who, then, is the greatest in the kingdom of heaven?" An argument started among the disciples as to which of them would be the greatest. Jesus, knowing their thoughts, took a little child whom He placed among them. Taking the child in His arms, He said to them, *"Truly I tell you, unless you change and become like little children, you will never enter the kingdom of heaven. Therefore, whoever takes the lowly position of this child is the greatest in the kingdom of heaven. And whoever welcomes one such child in my name welcomes me. Whoever welcomes me does not welcome me only, but the one who sent me. For it is the one who is least among you all who is the greatest."*—[Matthew 18:1-5, Mark 9:33-37, Luke 9:46-48]

TEMPTATIONS TO SIN

John said to him, "Teacher, we saw someone who doesn't follow us casting out demons in your name; and we forbade him, because he doesn't follow us."

But Jesus said, "Don't forbid him, for there is no one who will do a mighty work in my name and be able quickly to speak evil of me. For whoever is not against us is on our side. For whoever will give you a cup of water to drink in my name because you are Christ's, most certainly I tell you, he will in no way lose his reward.

And He said to His disciples, "Temptations to sin are sure to come, but woe to the one through whom they come! *"If anyone causes one of these little ones—those who believe in me—to stumble, it would be better for them if a large millstone were hung around their neck and they were thrown into the depths of the sea. Woe to the world because of the things that cause people to stumble! Such things must come, but woe to the person through whom they come!*

If your hand or your foot causes you to stumble, cut it off and throw it away. It is better for you to enter life maimed or crippled than to have two hands or two feet and be thrown into eternal fire, where the fire never goes out. And if your eye causes you to stumble, gouge it out and throw it away. It is better for you to enter life with one eye than to have two eyes and be thrown into hell, where 'the worms that eat them do not die, and the fire is not quenched.'

Everyone will be salted with fire. Salt is good, but if it loses its saltiness, how can you make it salty again? Have salt among yourselves, and be at peace with each other."—Matthew 18:6-9, Mark 9:38-50, Luke 9:49-50, and Luke 17:1-2]

PARABLE OF THE LOST SHEEP

See that you don't despise one of these little ones, for I tell you that in heaven their angels always see the face of my Father who is in heaven. For the Son of Man came to save that which was lost.

"What do you think? If a man has one hundred sheep, and one of them goes astray, doesn't he leave the ninety-nine, go to the mountains, and seek that which has gone astray? If he finds it, most assuredly I tell you, he rejoices over it more than over the ninety-nine which have not gone astray. Even so it is not the will of your Father who is in heaven that one of these little ones should perish.

He told them this parable. *"Which of you men, if you had one hundred sheep, and lost one of them, wouldn't leave the ninety-nine in the wilderness, and go after the one that was lost, until he found it? When he has found it, he carries it on his shoulders, rejoicing. When he comes home, he calls together his friends and his neighbors, saying to them, 'Rejoice with me, for I have found my sheep which was lost!' I tell you that even so there will be more joy in heaven over one sinner who repents, than over ninety-nine righteous people who need no repentance. Or what woman, if she had ten drachma coins, if she lost one drachma coin, wouldn't light a lamp, sweep the house, and seek diligently until she found it? When she has found it, she calls together her friends and neighbors, saying, 'Rejoice with me, for I have found the drachma which I had lost.' Even so, I tell you, there is joy in the presence of the angels of God over one sinner repenting."* —[Matthew 18:10-14, *Luke 15:3-10*]

IF YOUR BROTHER SINS AGAINST YOU

"Be on your guard! If your brother sins against you, rebuke him. Go, show him his fault between you and him alone. If he listens to you and repents, forgive him. And if he sends against you seven times a day, and returns to you seven times, saying, "I repent," you shall forgive him. You have gained back your brother. But if he doesn't listen, take one or two more with you, that at the mouth of two or three witnesses every word may be established. If he refuses to listen to them, tell it to the assembly. If he refuses to hear the assembly also, let him be to you as a Gentile or a tax collector. Most assuredly I tell you, whatever things you will bind on earth will be bound in heaven, and whatever things you will release on earth will be released in heaven. Again, assuredly I tell you, that if two of you will agree on earth concerning anything that they will ask, it will be done for them by my Father who is in heaven. For where two or three are gathered together in my name, there I am in the midst of them."—[Matthew 18:15-20, Luke 17:3-4] Messenger to Samaya, I will follow first nine 5162

PARABLE OF THE UNFORGIVING SERVANT

Then Peter came and said to Him, "Lord, how often shall my brother sin against me, and I forgive him? Until seven times?"

Jesus said to him, *"I don't tell you until seven times, but, until seventy times seven. Therefore the Kingdom of Heaven is like a certain king, who wanted to reconcile accounts with his servants. When he had begun to reconcile, one was brought to him who owed him <u>ten thousand talents.</u> But because he couldn't pay, his lord commanded him to be sold, with his wife, his children, and all that he had, and payment to be made. The servant therefore fell down and kneeled before him, saying, 'Lord, have patience with me, and I will repay you all!' The lord of that servant, being moved with compassion, released him, and forgave him the debt.*

"But that servant went out, and found one of his fellow servants, who owed him <u>one hundred denarii,</u> and he grabbed him, and took him by the throat, saying, 'Pay me what you owe!'

"So his fellow servant fell down at his feet and begged him, saying, 'Have patience with me, and I will repay you!' He would not, but went and cast him into prison, until he should pay back that which was due. So when his fellow servants saw what was done, they were exceedingly sorry, and came and told to their lord all that was done. Then his lord called him in, and said to him, 'You wicked servant! I forgave you all that debt, because you begged me. Shouldn't you also have had mercy on your fellow servant, even as I had mercy on you?' His lord was angry, and delivered him to the tormentors, until he should pay all that was due to him. So my heavenly Father will also do to you, if you don't each forgive your brother from your hearts for his misdeeds."—[Matthew 18:21-35]

THE RETURN of THE SEVENTY-TWO

The seventy-two returned with joy, saying, "Lord, even the demons are subject to us in Your name!" And He said to them, "I saw Satan fall like lightning from heaven. Behold, I have given you authority to tread on serpents and scorpions, and over all the power of the enemy, and nothing shall hurt you. Nevertheless, do not rejoice in this, that the spirits are subject to you, but rejoice that your names are written in heaven."—[Luke 10:17-20]

JESUS REJOICES IN THE FATHER'S WILL

In that same hour He rejoiced in the Holy Spirit and said, *"I thank you, Father, Lord of heaven and earth, that You have hidden these things from the wise and understanding and revealed them to little children; yes, Father, for such was Your gracious will. All things have been handed over to me by my Father, and no one knows who the Son is except the Father, or who the Father is except the Son and anyone to whom the Son chooses to reveal Him."* Then turning to the disciples He said privately, *"Blessed are the eyes that see what you see! For I tell you that many prophets and kings desired to see what you see, and did not see it, and to hear what you hear, and did not hear it."*—[Matthew 11:25-28, Luke 10:21-24]

THE PARABLE of the GOOD SAMARITAN

Behold, a certain lawyer stood up and tested Him, saying, "Teacher, what shall I do to inherit eternal life?"

He said to him, *"What is written in the law? How do you read it?"*

He answered, "You shall love the Lord your God with all your heart, with all your soul, with all your strength, and with all your mind; and your neighbor as yourself."

He said to him, *"You have answered correctly. Do this, and you will live."*

But he, desiring to justify himself, asked Jesus, "Who is my neighbor?"

Jesus answered, *"A certain man was going down from Jerusalem to Jericho, and he fell among robbers, who both stripped him and beat him, and departed, leaving him half dead. By chance a certain priest was going down that way. When he saw him, he passed by on the other side. In the same way a Levite also, when he came to the place, and saw him, passed by on the other side. But a certain Samaritan, as he traveled, came where he was. When he saw him, he was moved with compassion, came to him, and bound up his wounds, pouring on oil and wine. He set him on his own animal, and brought him to an inn, and took care of him. On the next day, when he departed, he took out two denarii, and gave them to the host, and said to him, 'Take care of him. Whatever you spend beyond that, I will repay you when I return.' Now which of these three do you think seemed to be a neighbor to him who fell among the robbers?"*

He said, "He who showed mercy on him."

Then Jesus said to him, *"Go and do likewise."*—[Luke 10:25-37]

MARTHA & MARY

It happened as they went on their way, Jesus entered into a certain village, and a certain woman named Martha received Him into her house. She had a sister called Mary, who also sat at Jesus' feet, and listened to what He taught. But Martha was distracted with much serving, and she came up to Him, and said, "Lord, don't you care that my sister left me to serve alone? Ask her therefore to help me."

Jesus answered her, *"Martha, Martha, you are anxious and troubled about many things, but one thing is needed. Mary has chosen the good part, which will not be taken away from her."*—[Luke 10:38-42]

THE LORD'S PRAYER

It happened that when He finished praying in a certain place, one of His disciples said to him, "Lord, teach us to pray, just as John also taught his disciples."

He said to them, *"When you pray, say,*

'Our Father in heaven,
  May Your name be kept holy.

May Your Kingdom come.
  May Your will be done on Earth, as it is in heaven.

Give us day by day our daily bread.

Forgive us our sins,
  For we ourselves also forgive everyone who is indebted to us.

Bring us not into temptation,
  But deliver us from the evil one.'"

He said to them, *"Which of you, if you go to a friend at midnight, and tell him, 'Friend, lend me three loaves of bread, for a friend of mine has come to me from a journey, and I have nothing to set before him,' and he from within will answer and say, 'Don't bother me. The door is now shut, and my children are with me in bed. I can't get up and give it to you'? I tell you, although he will not rise and give it to him because he is his friend, yet because of his persistence, he will get up and give him as many as he needs.*

"I tell you, keep asking, and it will be given you. Keep seeking, and you will find. Keep knocking, and it will be opened to you. For everyone who asks receives. He who seeks finds. To him who knocks it will be opened.

"Which of you fathers, if your son asks for bread, will give him a stone? Or if he asks for a fish, he won't give him a snake instead of a fish, will he? Or if he asks for an egg, he won't give him a scorpion, will he? If you then, being evil, know how to give good gifts to your children, how much more will your heavenly Father give the Holy Spirit to those who ask Him?"—[Luke 11:1-13]

BEWARE of the PHARISEE'S LEAVEN

Meanwhile, when a multitude of many thousands had gathered together, so much so that they trampled on each other, He began to tell His disciples first of all, *"Beware of the yeast of the Pharisees, which is hypocrisy. But there is nothing covered up, that will not be revealed, nor hidden, that will not be known. Therefore whatever you have said in the darkness will be heard in the light. What you have spoken in the ear in the inner chambers will be proclaimed on the housetops.*—[Luke 12:1-3]

HAVE NO FEAR

"I tell you, my friends, don't be afraid of those who kill the body, and after that have no more that they can do. But I will warn you whom you should fear. Fear Him, who after He has killed, has the power to cast into Gehenna. Yes, I tell you, fear Him.

"Aren't five sparrows sold for two assaria coins? Not one of them is forgotten by God. But the very hairs of your head are all numbered. Therefore don't be afraid. You are of more value than many sparrows.

"I tell you, everyone who confesses me before men, him will the Son of Man also confess before the angels of God; but he who denies me in the presence of men will be denied in the presence of the angels of God. Everyone who speaks a word against the Son of Man will be forgiven, but those who blaspheme against the Holy Spirit will not be forgiven. When they bring you before the synagogues, the rulers, and the authorities, don't be anxious how or what you will answer, or what you will say; for the Holy Spirit will teach you in that same hour what you must say."—[Luke 12:4-12]

THE PARABLE of the RICH FOOL

One of the multitude said to him, "Teacher, tell my brother to divide the inheritance with me."

But He said to him, *"Man, who made me a judge or an arbitrator over you?"* He said to them, *"Beware! Keep yourselves from covetousness, for a man's life doesn't consist of the abundance of the things which he possesses."*

He spoke a parable to them, saying, *"The ground of a certain rich man brought forth abundantly. He reasoned within himself, saying, 'What will I do, because I don't have room to store my crops?' He said, 'This is what I will do. I will pull down my barns, and build bigger ones, and there I will store all my grain and my goods. I will tell my soul, "Soul, you have many goods laid up for many years. Take your ease, eat, drink, be merry."'*

"But God said to him, 'You foolish one, tonight your soul is required of you. The things which you have prepared--whose will they be?' So is he who lays up treasure for himself, and is not rich toward God."—[Luke 12:13-21]

DO NOT BE ANXIOUS

He said to his disciples, *"Therefore I tell you, don't be anxious for your life, what you will eat, nor yet for your body, what you will wear. Life is more than food, and the body is more than clothing. Consider the ravens: they don't sow, they don't reap, they have no warehouse or barn, and God feeds them. How much more valuable are you than birds! Which of you by being anxious can add a cubit to his height? If then you aren't able to do even the least things, why are you anxious about the rest? Consider the lilies, how they grow. They don't toil, neither do they spin; yet I tell you, even Solomon in all his glory was not arrayed like one of these. But if this is how God clothes the grass in the field, which today exists, and tomorrow is cast into the oven, how much more will He clothe you, O you of little faith? Don't seek what you will eat or what you will drink; neither be anxious. For the nations of the world seek after all of these things, but your Father knows that you need these things. But seek God's Kingdom, and all these things will be added to you. Don't be afraid, little flock, for it is your Father's good pleasure to give you the Kingdom. Sell that which you have, and give gifts to the needy. Make for yourselves purses which don't grow old, a treasure in the heavens that doesn't fail, where no thief approaches, neither moth destroys. For where your treasure is, there will your heart be also.*—[Luke 12:22-34]

STAY READY

"Let your loins be girded and your lamps burning. Be like men watching for their lord, when he returns from the marriage feast; that, when he comes and knocks, they may immediately open to him. Blessed are those servants, whom the lord will find watching when he comes. Most assuredly I tell you, that he will dress himself, and make them recline, and will come and serve them. They will be blessed if he comes in the second or third watch, and finds them so. But know this, that if the master of the house had known in what hour the thief was coming, he would have watched, and not allowed his house to be broken into. Therefore be ready also, for the Son of Man is coming in an hour that you don't expect Him."

Peter said to him, "Lord, are You telling this parable to us, or to everybody?"

The Lord said, *"Who then is the faithful and wise steward, whom his lord will set over his household, to give them their portion of food at the right times? Blessed is that servant whom his lord will find doing so when he comes. Truly I tell you, that he will set him over all that he has. But if that servant says in his heart, 'My lord delays his coming,' and begins to beat the menservants and the maidservants, and to eat and drink, and to be drunken, then the lord of that servant will come in a day when he isn't expecting him, and in an hour that he doesn't know, and will cut him in two, and place his portion with the unfaithful. That servant, who knew his lord's will, and didn't prepare, nor do what he wanted, will be beaten with many stripes, but he who didn't know, and did things worthy of stripes, will be beaten with few stripes. To whoever much is given, of him will much be required; and to whom much was entrusted, of him more will be asked.*—[Luke 12:35-48]

NOT PEACE BUT DIVISION

"I came to throw fire on the earth. I wish it were already kindled. But I have a baptism to be baptized with, and how distressed I am until it is

accomplished! Do you think that I have come to give peace in the earth? I tell you, no, but rather division. For from now on, there will be five in one house divided, three against two, and two against three. They will be divided, father against son, and son against father; mother against daughter, and daughter against her mother; mother-in-law against her daughter-in-law, and daughter-in-law against her mother-in-law."—[Luke 12:49-53]

INTERPRETING THE TIME

He said to the multitudes also, *"When you see a cloud rising from the west, immediately you say, 'A shower is coming,' and so it happens. When a south wind blows, you say, 'There will be a scorching heat,' and it happens. You hypocrites! You know how to interpret the appearance of the earth and the sky, but how is it that you don't interpret this time?"* —[Luke 12:54-56]

SETTLING with YOUR ACCUSER

"Why don't you judge for yourselves what is right? For when you are going with your adversary before the magistrate, try diligently on the way to be released from him, lest perhaps he drag you to the judge, and the judge deliver you to the officer, and the officer throw you into prison. I tell you, you will by no means get out of there, until you have paid the very last penny."—[Luke 12:57-59]

REPENT OR PERISH

Now there were some present at the same time who told him about the Galileans, whose blood Pilate had mixed with their sacrifices. Jesus answered them, *"Do you think that these Galileans were worse sinners than all the other Galileans, because they suffered such things? I tell you, no, but, unless you repent, you will all perish in the same way. Or those eighteen, on whom the tower in Siloam fell, and killed them; do you think that they were worse offenders than all the men who dwell in Jerusalem? I tell you, no, but, unless you repent, you will all perish in the same way."*—[Luke 13:1-5]

THE PARABLE of the BARREN FIG TREE

He spoke this parable. *"A certain man had a fig tree planted in his vineyard, and he came seeking fruit on it, and found none. He said to the vine dresser, 'Behold, these three years I have come looking for fruit on this fig tree, and found none. Cut it down. Why does it waste the soil?' He answered, 'Lord, leave it alone this year also, until I dig around it, and fertilize it. If it bears fruit, fine; but if not, after that, you can cut it down.'"*—[Luke 13:6-9]

CHAPTER 15

SAMARITAN VILLAGE REJECTS JESUS

After these things, Jesus was walking in Galilee, for He wouldn't walk in Judea, because the Jews sought to kill Him. Now the feast of the Jews, the Feast of Booths, was at hand. His brothers therefore said to Him, "Depart from here, and go into Judea, that Your disciples also may see Your works which You do. For no one does anything in secret, and Himself seeks to be known openly. If You do these things, reveal Yourself to the world." For even His brothers didn't believe in Him.

Jesus therefore said to them, *"My time has not yet come, but your time is always ready. The world can't hate you, but it hates me, because I testify about it, that its works are evil. You go up to the feast. I am not yet going up to this feast, because my time is not yet fulfilled."*

Having said these things to them, He stayed in Galilee. But when his brothers had gone up to the feast, then He also went up, not publicly, but as it were in secret.

The Jews therefore sought Him at the feast, and said, "Where is He?" There was much murmuring among the multitudes concerning Him. Some said, "He is a good man." Others said, "Not so, but He leads the multitude astray." Yet no one spoke openly of Him for fear of the Jews.

It came to pass, when the days were near that He should be taken up, He intently set His face to go to Jerusalem, and sent messengers before His face. They went, and entered into a village of the Samaritans, so as to prepare for Him. They didn't receive Him, because He was traveling with His face set towards Jerusalem. When His disciples, James and John, saw this, they said, "Lord, do You want us to command fire to come down from the sky, and destroy them, just as Elijah did?"

But He turned and rebuked them, *"You don't know of what kind of spirit you are. For the Son of Man didn't come to destroy men's lives, but to save them."*

They went to another village.—[Luke 9:51-56 and John 7:1-10]

COULD A DEMON-POSSESSED MAN HEAL THE BLIND

When it was now the midst of the feast, Jesus went up into the temple and taught. The Jews therefore marveled, saying, "How does this man know letters, having never been educated?"

Jesus therefore answered them, *"My teaching is not mine, but His who sent me. If anyone desires to do His will, he will know about the teaching, whether it is from God, or if I am speaking from myself. He who speaks from himself seeks his own glory, but he who seeks the glory of Him who sent him, the same is true, and no unrighteousness is in him. Didn't Moses give you the law, and yet none of you keeps the law? Why do you seek to kill me?"*

The multitude answered, "You have a demon! Who seeks to kill You?"

Jesus answered them, *"I did one work, and you all marvel because of it. Moses has given you circumcision (not that it is of Moses, but of the fathers), and on the Sabbath you circumcise a boy. If a boy receives circumcision on the Sabbath, that the law of Moses may not be broken, are you angry with me, because I made a man every bit whole on the Sabbath? Don't judge according to appearance, but judge righteous judgment."*

Therefore some of them of Jerusalem said, "Isn't this He whom they seek to kill? Behold, He speaks openly, and they say nothing to Him. Can it be that the rulers indeed know that this is truly the Christ? However we know where this man comes from, but when the Christ comes, no one will know where He comes from."

Jesus therefore cried out in the temple, teaching and saying, *"You both know me, and know where I am from. I have not come of myself, but He who sent me is true, whom you don't know. I know Him, because I am from Him, and He sent me."*

They sought therefore to take Him; but no one laid a hand on Him, because His hour had not yet come. But of the multitude, many believed in Him.

They said, "When the Christ comes, He won't do more signs than those which this man has done, will He?" The Pharisees heard the multitude murmuring these things concerning Him, and the chief priests and the Pharisees sent officers to arrest Him.

Then Jesus said, *"I will be with you a little while longer, then I go to Him who sent me. You will seek me, and won't find me; and where I am, you can't come."*

The Jews therefore said among themselves, "Where will this man go that we won't find Him? Will He go to the Dispersion among the Greeks, and teach the Greeks? What is this word that He said, *'You will seek me, and won't find me; and where I am, you can't come?'"*

Now on the last and greatest day of the feast, Jesus stood and cried out, *"If anyone is thirsty, let him come to me and drink! He who believes in me, as the Scripture has said, from within him will flow rivers of living water."* But He said this about the Spirit, which those believing in Him were to receive. For the Holy Spirit was not yet given, because Jesus wasn't yet glorified.

Many of the multitude therefore, when they heard these words, said, "This is truly the prophet." Others said, "This is the Christ." But some said, "What, does the Christ come out of Galilee?! Hasn't the Scripture said that the Christ comes of the seed of David, and from Bethlehem, the village where David was?" So there arose a division in the multitude because of Him. Some of them would have arrested Him, but no one laid hands on Him. The officers therefore came to the chief priests and Pharisees, and they said to them, "Why didn't you bring Him?"

The officers answered, "No man ever spoke like this man!"

The Pharisees therefore answered them, "You aren't also led astray, are you? Have any of the rulers believed in Him, or of the Pharisees? But this multitude that doesn't know the law is accursed."

Nicodemus (he who came to Him by night, being one of them) said to them, "Does our law judge a man, unless it first hears from him personally and knows what he does?"

They answered him, "Are you also from Galilee? Search, and see that no prophet has arisen out of Galilee."

Everyone went to his own house, but Jesus went to the Mount of Olives. Now very early in the morning, He came again into the temple, and all the people came to Him. He sat down, and taught them. The scribes and the Pharisees brought a woman taken in adultery. Having set her in the midst, they told Him, "Teacher, we found this woman in adultery, in the very act. Now in our law, Moses commanded us to stone such. What then do You say about her?" They said this testing Him, that they might have something to accuse Him of.

But Jesus stooped down, and wrote on the ground with His finger. But when they continued asking Him, he looked up and said to them, *"He who is without sin among you, let him throw the first stone at her."* Again he stooped down, and with his finger wrote on the ground.

They, when they heard it, being convicted by their conscience, went out one by one, beginning from the oldest, even to the last. Jesus was left alone with the woman where she was, in the middle. Jesus, standing up, saw her and said, *"Woman, where are your accusers? Did no one condemn you?"*

She said, "No one, Lord."

Jesus said, *"Neither do I condemn you. Go your way. From now on, sin no more."*

Again, therefore, Jesus spoke to them, saying, *"I am the light of the world. He who follows me will not walk in the darkness, but will have the light of life."*

The Pharisees therefore said to Him, "You testify about Yourself. Your testimony is not valid."

Jesus answered them, *"Even if I testify about myself, my testimony is true, for I know where I came from, and where I am going; but you don't know where I came from, or where I am going. You judge according to the flesh. I judge no one. Even if I do judge, my judgment is true, for I am not alone, but I am with the Father who sent me. It's also written in your law that the testimony of two people is valid. I am one who testifies about myself, and the Father who sent me testifies about me."*

They said therefore to Him, "Where is your Father?"

Jesus answered, *"You know neither me, nor my Father. If you knew me, you would know my Father also."* Jesus spoke these words in the treasury, as He taught in the temple. Yet no one arrested Him, because His hour had not yet come. Jesus said therefore again to them, *"I am going away, and you will seek me, and you will die in your sins. Where I go, you can't come."*

The Jews therefore said, "Will He kill himself, that He says, *'Where I am going, you can't come?'"*

He said to them, *"You are from beneath. I am from above. You are of this world. I am not of this world. I said therefore to you that you will die in your sins; for unless you believe that I am He, you will die in your sins."*

They said therefore to Him, "Who are you?"

Jesus said to them, *"Just what I have been saying to you from the beginning. I have many things to speak and to judge concerning you. However He who sent me is true; and the things which I heard from Him, these I say to the world."*

They didn't understand that He spoke to them about the Father. Jesus therefore said to them, *"When you have lifted up the Son of Man, then you will know that I am He, and I do nothing of myself, but as my Father taught me, I say these things. He who sent me is with me. The Father hasn't left me alone, for I always do the things that are pleasing to him."*

As He spoke these things, many believed in Him. Jesus therefore said to those Jews who had believed Him, *"If you remain in my word, then you are truly my disciples. You will know the truth, and the truth will make you free."*

They answered Him, "We are Abraham's seed, and have never been in bondage to anyone. How do you say, *'You will be made free?'"*

Jesus answered them, *"Most assuredly I tell you, everyone who commits sin is the bondservant of sin. A bondservant doesn't live in the house forever. A son remains forever. If therefore the Son makes you free, you will be free indeed. I know that you are Abraham's seed, yet you seek to kill me, because my word finds no place in you. I say the things which I have seen with my Father; and you also do the things which you have seen with your father."*

They answered Him, "Our father is Abraham."

Jesus said to them, *"If you were Abraham's children, you would do the works of Abraham. But now you seek to kill me, a man who has told you the truth, which I heard from God. Abraham didn't do this. You do the works of your father."*

They said to Him, "We were not born of sexual immorality. We have one Father, God."

Therefore Jesus said to them, *"If God were your Father, you would love me, for I came out and have come from God. For I haven't come of myself, but He sent me. Why don't you understand my speech? Because you can't hear my word. You are of your Father, the devil, and you want to do the desires of your father. He was a murderer from the beginning, and doesn't stand in the truth, because there is no truth in him. When he speaks a lie, he speaks on his own; for he is a liar, and the father of it. But because I tell the truth, you don't believe me. Which of you convicts me of sin? If I tell the truth, why do you not believe me? He who is of God hears the words of God. For this cause you don't hear, because you are not of God."*

Then the Jews answered Him, "Don't we say well that You are a Samaritan, and have a demon?"

Jesus answered, *"I don't have a demon, but I honor my Father, and you dishonor me. But I don't seek my own glory. There is one who seeks and judges. Most assuredly, I tell you, if a person keeps my word, he will never see death."*

Then the Jews said to Him, "Now we know that You have a demon. Abraham died, and the prophets; and You say, *'If a man keeps my word, he will never taste of death.'* Are You greater than our father, Abraham, who died? The prophets died. Who do You make Yourself out to be?"

Jesus answered, *"If I glorify myself, my glory is nothing. It is my Father who glorifies me, of whom you say that He is our God. You have not known Him, but I know Him. If I said, 'I don't know Him,' I would be like you, a liar. But I know Him, and keep His word. Your father Abraham rejoiced to see my day. He saw it, and was glad."*

The Jews therefore said to Him, "You are not yet fifty years old, and have You seen Abraham?"

Jesus said to them, *"Most assuredly, I tell you, before Abraham came into existence, I AM."*

Therefore they took up stones to throw at Him, but Jesus was hidden, and went out of the temple, having gone through the midst of them, and so passed by.

As He passed by, He saw a man blind from birth. His disciples asked Him, "Rabbi, who sinned, this man or his parents, that he was born blind?"

Jesus answered, *"Neither did this man sin, nor his parents; but, that the works of God might be revealed in him. I must work the works of Him who sent me, while it is day. The night is coming, when no one can work. While I am in the world, I am the light of the world."* When He had said this, He spat on the ground, made mud with the saliva, anointed the blind man's eyes with the mud, and said to him, *"Go, wash in the pool of Siloam"* (which means "Sent"). So he went away, washed, and came back seeing. The neighbors therefore, and those who saw that he was blind before, said, "Isn't this he who sat and begged?" Others were saying, "It is he." Still others were saying, "He looks like him.

He said, "I am he." They therefore were asking him, "How were your eyes opened?"

He answered, "A man called Jesus made mud, anointed my eyes, and said to me, *'Go to the pool of Siloam, and wash.'* So I went away and washed, and I received sight."

Then they asked him, "Where is He?"

He said, "I don't know."

They brought him who had been blind to the Pharisees. It was a Sabbath when Jesus made the mud and opened his eyes. Again therefore the Pharisees also asked him how he received his sight. He said to them, "He put mud on my eyes, I washed, and I see."

Some of the Pharisees therefore said, "This man is not from God, because He doesn't keep the Sabbath." Others said, "How can a man who is a sinner do such signs?" There was division among them. Therefore they asked the blind man again, "What do you say about Him, because He opened your eyes?"

He said, "He is a prophet."

The Jews therefore did not believe concerning him, that he had been blind, and had received his sight, until they called the parents of him who had received his sight, and asked them, "Is this your son, who you say was born blind? How then does he now see?"

His parents answered them, "We know that this is our son, and that he was born blind; but how he now sees, we don't know; or who opened his eyes, we don't know. He is of age. Ask him. He will speak for himself." His parents said these things because they feared the Jews; for the Jews had already agreed that if any man would confess Him as Christ, he would be put out of the synagogue. Therefore his parents said, "He is of age. Ask him."

So they called the man who was blind a second time, and said to him, "Give glory to God. We know that this man is a sinner."

He therefore answered, "I don't know if He is a sinner. One thing I do know: that though I was blind, now I see."

They said to him again, "What did He do to you? How did He open your eyes?"

He answered them, "I told you already, and you didn't listen. Why do you want to hear it again? You don't also want to become His disciples, do you?"

They insulted him and said, "You are His disciple, but we are disciples of Moses. We know that God has spoken to Moses. But as for this man, we don't know where He comes from."

The man answered them, "How amazing! You don't know where He comes from, yet He opened my eyes. We know that God doesn't listen to sinners, but if anyone is a worshiper of God, and does His will, He listens to Him. Since the world began it has never been heard of that anyone opened the eyes of someone born blind. If this man were not from God, He could do nothing."

They answered him, "You were altogether born in sins, and do you teach us?" They threw him out.

Jesus heard that they had thrown him out, and finding him, He said, *"Do you believe in the Son of God?"*

He answered, "Who is He, Lord, that I may believe in Him?"

Jesus said to him, *"You have both seen Him, and it is He who speaks with you."*

He said, "Lord, I believe!" and he worshiped Him.

Jesus said, *"I came into this world for judgment, that those who don't see may see; and that those who see may become blind."*

Those of the Pharisees who were with Him heard these things, and said to Him, "Are we also blind?"

Jesus said to them, *"If you were blind, you would have no sin; but now you say, 'We see.' Therefore your sin remains.*

"Most assuredly, I tell you, one who doesn't enter by the door into the sheep fold, but climbs up some other way, the same is a thief and a robber. But one who enters in by the door is the shepherd of the sheep. The gatekeeper opens the gate for him, and the sheep listen to his voice. He calls his own sheep by name, and leads them out. Whenever he brings out his own sheep, he goes before them, and the sheep follow him, for they know his voice. They will by no means follow a stranger, but will flee from him; for they don't know the voice of strangers." Jesus spoke this parable to them, but they didn't understand what He was telling them.

Jesus therefore said to them again, *"Most assuredly, I tell you, I am the sheep's door. All who came before me are thieves and robbers, but the sheep didn't listen to them. I am the door. If anyone enters in by me, he will be saved, and will go in and go out, and will find pasture. The thief only comes to steal, kill, and destroy. I came that they may have life, and may have it abundantly. I am the good shepherd. The good shepherd lays down his life for the sheep. He who is a hired hand, and not a shepherd, who doesn't own the sheep, sees the wolf coming, leaves the sheep, and flees. The wolf snatches the sheep, and scatters them. The hired hand flees because he is a hired hand, and doesn't care for the sheep. I am the good shepherd. I know my own, and I'm known by my own; even as the Father knows me, and I know the Father. I lay down my life for the sheep. I have other sheep, which are not of this fold. I must bring them also, and they will hear my voice. They will become one flock with one shepherd. Therefore the Father loves me, because I lay down my life, that I may take it again. No one takes it away from me, but I lay it down by myself. I have power to lay it down, and I have power to take it again. I received this commandment from my Father."*

Therefore a division arose again among the Jews because of these words. Many of them said, "He has a demon, and is insane! Why do you listen to Him?" Others said, "These are not the sayings of one possessed by a demon.

It isn't possible for a demon to open the eyes of the blind, is it?"—[John 7:11-10:21]

CHAPTER 16

A WOMAN with A DISABLING SPIRIT

He was teaching in one of the synagogues on the Sabbath day. Behold, there was a woman who had a spirit of infirmity eighteen years, and she was bent over, and could in no way straighten herself up. When Jesus saw her, He called her, and said to her, *"Woman, you are freed from your infirmity."* He laid His hands on her, and immediately she stood up straight, and glorified God.

The ruler of the synagogue, being indignant because Jesus had healed on the Sabbath, said to the multitude, "There are six days in which men ought to work. Therefore come on those days and be healed, and not on the Sabbath day!"

Therefore the Lord answered him, *"You hypocrites! Doesn't each one of you free his ox or his donkey from the stall on the Sabbath, and lead him away to water? Ought not this woman, being a daughter of Abraham, whom Satan had bound eighteen long years, be freed from this bondage on the Sabbath day?"*

As He said these things, all His adversaries were disappointed, and all the multitude rejoiced for all the glorious things that were done by Him.—[Luke 13:10-17]

THE MUSTARD SEED and the LEAVEN

He said, *"What is the Kingdom of God like? To what shall I compare it? It is like a grain of mustard seed, which a man took, and put in his own garden. It grew, and became a large tree, and the birds of the sky lodged in its branches."*

Again He said, "To what shall I compare the Kingdom of God? It is like yeast, which a woman took and hid in <u>three measures</u> of flour, until it was all leavened."—[Luke 13:18-21]

He went through the cities and villages, teaching, and journeying toward Jerusalem. And someone said to Him, "Lord, will there be few who are saved?" And He said to them, *"Strive to enter through the narrow gate, for many, I say to you, will seek to enter and will not be able.*

"When once the Master of the house has risen up and shut the door, and you begin to stand outside and knock at the door, saying, 'Lord, Lord, open for us,' then He will answer and say to you, 'I do not know you, where you are from.' Then you will begin to say, 'We ate and drank in Your presence, and You taught in our streets.' But He will say, 'I tell you I do not know you, where you are from. Depart from Me, all you workers of iniquity.'

There will be weeping and gnashing of teeth, when you see Abraham and Isaac and Jacob and all the prophets in the kingdom of God, and yourselves thrust out. They will come from the east and the west, from the north and the south, and sit down in the kingdom of God. And indeed some are last who will be first there, and there are some who are first now, who will be last." [Luke 13:22-30]

At that time some Pharisees said to him, "Get away from here if you want to live because Herod Antipas wants to kill you!" Jesus replied, *"Go tell that fox that I will keep on casting out demons and healing people today and tomorrow; and the third day I will accomplish my purpose.*

Yes, today, tomorrow, and the next day I must proceed on my way. For it wouldn't do for a prophet of God to be killed except in Jerusalem!"

(Matt. 23:37–39)

"O Jerusalem, Jerusalem, the city that kills the prophets and stones God's messengers! How often I have wanted to gather your children together as a hen protects her chicks beneath her wings, but you wouldn't let me.

And now, look, your house is abandoned. And you will never see me again until you say, 'Blessings on the one who comes in the name of the LORD!' [Luke 13:31-35]

When he went into the house of one of the rulers of the Pharisees on a Sabbath to eat bread, they were watching him. Behold, a certain man who had dropsy was in front of him. Jesus, answering, spoke to the lawyers and Pharisees, saying, "Is it lawful to heal on the Sabbath?"

But they were silent.

He took him, and healed him, and let him go. He answered them, "Which of you, if your son[a] or an ox fell into a well, wouldn't immediately pull him out on a Sabbath day?"

They couldn't answer him regarding these things.

He spoke a parable to those who were invited, when he noticed how they chose the best seats, and said to them, "When you are invited by anyone to a wedding feast, don't sit in the best seat, since perhaps someone more honorable than you might be invited by him, and he who invited both of you would come and tell you, 'Make room for this person.' Then you would begin, with shame, to take the lowest place. But when you are invited, go and sit in the lowest place, so that when he who invited you comes, he may tell you, 'Friend, move up higher.' Then you will be honored in the presence of all who sit at the table with you. For everyone who exalts himself will be humbled, and whoever humbles himself will be exalted."

He also said to the one who had invited him, "When you make a dinner or a supper, don't call your friends, nor your brothers, nor your kinsmen, nor rich neighbors, or perhaps they might also return the favor, and pay you back. But when you make a feast, ask the poor, the maimed, the lame, or the blind; and you will be blessed, because they don't have the resources to repay you. For you will be repaid in the resurrection of the righteous."

When one of those who sat at the table with him heard these things, he said to him, "Blessed is he who will feast in God's Kingdom!"

But he said to him, "A certain man made a great supper, and he invited many people. He sent out his servant at supper time to tell those who were invited, 'Come, for everything is ready now.' They all as one began to make excuses.

"The first said to him, 'I have bought a field, and I must go and see it. Please have me excused.'

"Another said, 'I have bought five yoke of oxen, and I must go try them out. Please have me excused.'

"Another said, 'I have married a wife, and therefore I can't come.'

"That servant came, and told his lord these things. Then the master of the house, being angry, said to his servant, 'Go out quickly into the streets and lanes of the city, and bring in the poor, maimed, blind, and lame.'

"The servant said, 'Lord, it is done as you commanded, and there is still room.'

"The lord said to the servant, 'Go out into the highways and hedges, and compel them to come in, that my house may be filled. For I tell you that none of those men who were invited will taste of my supper.'"

Now great multitudes were going with him. He turned and said to them, "If anyone comes to me, and doesn't disregard[b] his own father, mother, wife, children, brothers, and sisters, yes, and his own life also, he can't be my disciple. Whoever doesn't bear his own cross, and come after me, can't be my disciple. For which of you, desiring to build a tower, doesn't first sit down and count the cost, to see if he has enough to complete it? Or perhaps, when he has laid a foundation, and is not able to finish, everyone who sees begins to mock him, saying, 'This man began to build, and wasn't able to finish.' Or what king, as he goes to encounter another king in war, will not sit down first and consider whether he is able with ten thousand to meet him who comes against him with twenty thousand? Or else, while the other is yet a great way off, he sends an envoy, and asks for conditions of peace. So therefore whoever of you who doesn't renounce all that he has, he can't be my disciple. Salt is good, but if the salt becomes flat and tasteless, with what do you season it? It is fit neither for the soil nor for the manure pile. It is thrown out. He who has ears to hear, let him hear."—[Luke 14:1-35]

THE FATHER and I ARE ONE

It was the Feast of the Dedication at Jerusalem. This took place in the winter, and Jesus was walking in the temple, in Solomon's porch. The Jews therefore came around Him and said to Him, "How long will you hold us in suspense? If you are the Christ, tell us plainly."

Jesus answered them, *"I told you, and you don't believe. The works that I do in my Father's name, these testify about me. But you don't believe, because you are not of my sheep, as I told you. My sheep hear my voice, and I know them, and they follow me. I give eternal life to them. They will never perish, and no one will snatch them out of my hand. My Father, who has given them to me, is greater than all. No one is able to snatch them out of my Father's hand. I and the Father are one."*

Therefore Jews took up stones again to stone Him. Jesus answered them, *"I have shown you many good works from my Father. For which of those works do you stone me?"*

The Jews answered Him, "We don't stone You for a good work, but for blasphemy: because You, being a man, make Yourself God."

Jesus answered them, *"Isn't it written in your law, 'I said, you are gods?' If He called them gods, to whom the word of God came (and the Scripture can't be broken), Do you say of Him whom the Father sanctified and sent into the world, 'You blaspheme,' because I said, 'I am the Son of God?' If I don't do the works of my Father, don't believe me. But if I do them, though you don't believe me, believe the works; that you may know and believe that the Father is in me, and I in the Father."*

They sought again to seize Him, and He went out of their hand. He went away again beyond the Jordan into the place where John was baptizing at first, and there He stayed. Many came to Him. They said, "John indeed did no sign, but everything that John said about this man is true." Many believed in Him there.—[John 10:22-42]

Now all the tax collectors and sinners were coming close to him to hear him. The Pharisees and the scribes murmured, saying, "This man welcomes sinners, and eats with them." He told them this parable. "Which of you men, if you had one hundred sheep, and lost one of them, wouldn't leave the ninety-nine in the wilderness, and go after the one that was lost, until he found it? When he has found it, he carries it on his shoulders, rejoicing.

When he comes home, he calls together his friends and his neighbors, saying to them, 'Rejoice with me, for I have found my sheep which was lost!' I tell you that even so there will be more joy in heaven over one sinner who repents, than over ninety-nine righteous people who need no repentance. Or what woman, if she had ten drachma {A drachma coin was worth about 2 days wages for an agricultural laborer.} coins, if she lost one drachma coin, wouldn't light a lamp, sweep the house, and seek diligently until she found it?

When she has found it, she calls together her friends and neighbors, saying, 'Rejoice with me, for I have found the drachma which I had lost.' Even so, I tell you, there is joy in the presence of the angels of God over one sinner repenting." He said, "A certain man had two sons. The younger of them said to his father, 'Father, give me my share of your property.' He divided his livelihood between them. Not many days after, the younger son gathered all of this together and traveled into a far country. There he wasted his property with riotous living.

When he had spent all of it, there arose a severe famine in that country, and he began to be in need. He went and joined himself to one of the citizens of that country, and he sent him into his fields to feed pigs. He wanted to fill his belly with the husks that the pigs ate, but no one gave him any. But when he came to himself he said, 'How many hired servants of my father's have bread enough to spare, and I'm dying with hunger!

I will get up and go to my father, and will tell him, "Father, I have sinned against heaven, and in your sight. I am no more worthy to be called your son. Make me as one of your hired servants." He arose, and came to his father. But while he was still far off, his father saw him, and was moved with compassion, and ran, and fell on his neck, and kissed him. The son said to him, 'Father, I have sinned against heaven, and in your sight. I am no longer worthy to be called your son.' But the father said to his servants, 'Bring out the best robe, and put it on him. Put a ring on his hand, and shoes on his feet. Bring the fattened calf, kill it, and let us eat, and celebrate; for this, my son, was dead, and is alive again. He was lost, and is found.' They began to celebrate.

"Now his elder son was in the field. As he came near the house, he heard music and dancing. He called one of the servants to him, and asked what was going on. He said to him, 'Your brother has come, and your father has killed the fattened calf, because he has received him back safe and healthy.' But he was angry, and would not go in. Therefore his father came out, and begged him. But he answered his father, 'Behold, these many years I have served you, and I never disobeyed a commandment of yours, but you never gave me a goat, that I might celebrate with my friends.

But when this, your son, came, who has devoured your living with prostitutes, you killed the fattened calf for him.' He said to him, 'Son, you are always with me, and all that is mine is yours. But it was appropriate to celebrate and be glad, for this, your brother, was dead, and is alive again. He was lost, and is found.'

He also said to his disciples, "There was a certain rich man who had a manager. An accusation was made to him that this man was wasting his possessions. He called him, and said to him, 'What is this that I hear about you? Give an accounting of your management, for you can no longer be manager.'

The manager said within himself, 'What will I do, seeing that my lord is taking away the management position from me? I don't have the strength to dig. I am ashamed to beg. I know what I will do, so that when I am removed from management, they may receive me into their houses.' Calling each one of his lord's debtors to him, he said to the first, 'How much do you owe to my lord?' He said, 'A hundred batos of oil.' He said to him, 'Take your bill, and sit down quickly and write fifty.' Then he said to another, 'How much do you owe?' He said, 'A hundred cors of wheat.' He said to him, 'Take your bill, and write eighty.'

"His lord commended the dishonest manager because he had done wisely, for the children of this world are, in their own generation, wiser than the children of the light. I tell you, make for yourselves friends by means of unrighteous mammon, so that when you fail, they may receive you into the eternal tents. He who is faithful in a very little is faithful also in much. He who is dishonest in a very little is also dishonest in much. If therefore you have not been faithful in the unrighteous mammon, who will commit to your trust the true riches? If you have not been faithful in that which is another's, who will give you that which is your own? No servant can serve two masters, for either he will hate the one, and love the other; or else he will hold to one, and despise the other. You aren't able to serve God and Mammon."

The Pharisees, who were lovers of money, also heard all these things, and they scoffed at him. He said to them, "You are those who justify yourselves in the sight of men, but God knows your hearts. For that which is exalted among men is an abomination in the sight of God. The law and the prophets were until John. From that time the Good News of God's Kingdom is preached, and everyone is forcing his way into it. But it is easier for heaven and earth to pass away than for one tiny stroke of a pen in the law to fall. Everyone who divorces his wife and marries another commits adultery. He who marries one who is divorced from a husband commits adultery.

"Now there was a certain rich man, and he was clothed in purple and fine linen, living in luxury every day. A certain beggar, named Lazarus, was taken to his gate, full of sores, and desiring to be fed with the crumbs that fell from the rich man's table. Yes, even the dogs came and licked his sores. The beggar died, and he was carried away by the angels to Abraham's bosom. The rich man also died, and was buried. In Hades, he lifted up his eyes, being in torment, and saw Abraham far off, and Lazarus at his bosom. He cried and said, 'Father Abraham, have mercy on me, and send Lazarus, that he may dip the tip of his finger in water, and cool my tongue! For I am in anguish in this flame.'

"But Abraham said, 'Son, remember that you, in your lifetime, received your good things, and Lazarus, in the same way, bad things. But here he is now comforted, and you are in anguish. Besides all this, between us and you there is a great gulf fixed, that those who want to pass from here to you are not able, and that no one may cross over from there to us.'

"He said, 'I ask you therefore, father, that you would send him to my father's house; for I have five brothers, that he may testify to them, so they won't also come into this place of torment.' But Abraham said to him, 'They have Moses and the prophets. Let them listen to them.' He said, 'No, father Abraham, but if one goes to them from the dead, they will repent.' He said to him, 'If they don't listen to Moses and the prophets, neither will they be persuaded if one rises from the dead.' [Luke 15-16]

LAZARUS

Now a certain man was sick, Lazarus from Bethany, of the village of Mary and her sister, Martha. It was that Mary who had anointed the Lord with ointment and wiped His feet with her hair, whose brother, Lazarus, was sick. The sisters therefore sent to Him, saying, "Lord, behold, he for whom you have great affection is sick." But when Jesus heard it, He said, "This sickness is not to death, but for the glory of God, that God's Son may be glorified by it." Now Jesus loved Martha, and her sister, and Lazarus. When therefore He heard that he was sick, He stayed two days in the place where he was. Then after this He said to the disciples, *"Let's go into Judea again."*

The disciples asked Him, "Rabbi, the Jews were just trying to stone You. Are You going there again?"

Jesus answered, *"Aren't there twelve hours of daylight? If a man walks in the day, he doesn't stumble, because he sees the light of this world. But if a man walks in the night, he stumbles, because the light isn't in him."* He said these things, and after that, He said to them, *"Our friend, Lazarus, has fallen asleep, but I am going so that I may awake him out of sleep."*

The disciples therefore said, "Lord, if He has fallen asleep, He will recover."

Now Jesus had spoken of His death, but they thought that He spoke of taking rest in sleep. So Jesus said to them plainly then, *"Lazarus is dead. I am glad for your sakes that I was not there, so that you may believe. Nevertheless, let's go to him."*

Thomas therefore, who is called Didymus, said to his fellow disciples, "Let's go also, that we may die with him."—[John 11:1-16]

THE RESURRECTION and the LIFE

So when Jesus came, He found that he had been in the tomb four days already. Now Bethany was near Jerusalem, about fifteen stadia away. Many of the Jews had joined the women around Martha and Mary, to console them concerning their brother. Then when Martha heard that Jesus was coming, she went and met Him, but Mary stayed in the house. Therefore Martha said to Jesus, "Lord, if You would have been here, my brother wouldn't have died. Even now I know that whatever you ask of God, God will give You." Jesus said to her, "Your brother will rise again."

Martha said to Him, "I know that he will rise again in the resurrection at the last day."

Jesus said to her, *"I am the resurrection and the life. He who believes in me will still live, even if he dies. Whoever lives and believes in me will never die. Do you believe this?"*

She said to Him, "Yes, Lord. I have come to believe that You are the Christ, God's Son, He who comes into the world."

When she had said this, she went away and called Mary, her sister, secretly, saying, "The Teacher is here and is calling you."

When she heard this, she arose quickly and went to Him. Now Jesus had not yet come into the village, but was in the place where Martha met Him. Then the Jews who were with her in the house and were consoling her, when they saw Mary, that she rose up quickly and went out, followed her, saying, "She is going to the tomb to weep there." Therefore when Mary came to where Jesus was and saw Him, she fell down at His feet, saying to Him, "Lord, if You would have been here, my brother wouldn't have died."

When Jesus therefore saw her weeping, and the Jews weeping who came with her, He groaned in the spirit, and was troubled, and said, *"Where have you laid him?"*

They told him, "Lord, come and see."

Jesus wept.

The Jews therefore said, "See how much affection He had for him!" Some of them said, "Couldn't this man, who opened the eyes of him who was blind, have also kept this man from dying?"

Jesus therefore, again groaning in Himself, came to the tomb. Now it was a cave, and a stone lay against it. Jesus said, *"Take away the stone."*

Martha, the sister of him who was dead, said to Him, "Lord, by this time there is a stench, for He has been dead four days."

Jesus said to her, *"Didn't I tell you that if you believed, you would see God's glory?"*

So they took away the stone from the place where the dead man was lying.[c] Jesus lifted up His eyes, and said, *"Father, I thank You that You listened to me. I know that You always listen to me, but because of the multitude standing around I said this, that they may believe that You sent me."* When He had said this, He cried with a loud voice, *"Lazarus, come out!"*

He who was dead came out, bound hand and foot with wrappings, and His face was wrapped around with a cloth.

Jesus said to them, *"Free him, and let him go."*

Therefore many of the Jews who came to Mary and saw what Jesus did believed in Him. But some of them went away to the Pharisees and told them the things which Jesus had done. The chief priests therefore and the Pharisees gathered a council, and said, "What are we doing? For this man does many signs. If we leave Him alone like this, everyone will believe in Him, and the Romans will come and take away both our place and our nation."

But a certain one of them, Caiaphas, being high priest that year, said to them, "You know nothing at all, nor do you consider that it is advantageous for us that one man should die for the people, and that the whole nation not perish." Now he didn't say this of himself, but being high priest that year, he prophesied that Jesus would die for the nation, and not for the nation only, but that He might also gather together into one the children of God who are scattered abroad. So from that day forward they took counsel that they might put him to death. Jesus therefore walked no more openly among the Jews, but departed from there into the country near the wilderness, to a city called Ephraim. He stayed there with His disciples.—[John 11:17-54]

JESUS HEALS TEN LEPERS

It happened as He was on His way to Jerusalem, that He was passing along the borders of Samaria and Galilee. As He entered into a certain village, ten men who were lepers met Him, who stood at a distance. They lifted up their voices, saying, "Jesus, Master, have mercy on us!"

When He saw them, He said to them, *"Go and show yourselves to the priests."* It happened that as they went, they were cleansed. One of them, when he saw that he was healed, turned back, glorifying God with a loud voice. He fell on his face at Jesus' feet, giving Him thanks; and he was a Samaritan. Jesus answered, *"Weren't the ten cleansed? But where are the nine? Were there none found who returned to give glory to God, except this stranger?"* Then He said to Him, *"Get up, and go your way. Your faith has healed you."*—[Luke 17:11-19]

THE COMING of the KINGDOM

Being asked by the Pharisees when the Kingdom of God would come, He answered them, *"The Kingdom of God doesn't come with observation; neither will they say, 'Look, here!' or, 'Look, there!' for behold, the Kingdom of God is within you."*

He said to the disciples, *"The days will come, when you will desire to see one of the days of the Son of Man, and you will not see it. They will tell you, 'Look, here!' or 'Look, there!' Don't go away, nor follow after them, for as the lightning, when it flashes out of the one part under the sky, shines to the other part under the sky; so will the Son of Man be in his day. But first, He must suffer many things and be rejected by this generation. As it happened in the days of Noah, even so will it be also in the days of the Son of Man. They ate, they drank, they married, they were given in marriage, until the day that Noah entered into the ark, and the flood came, and destroyed them all. Likewise, even as it happened in the days of Lot: they ate, they drank, they bought, they sold, they planted, they built; but in the day that Lot went out from Sodom, it rained fire and sulfur from the sky, and destroyed them all. It will be the same way in the day that the Son of Man is revealed. In that day, he who will be on the housetop, and his goods in the house, let him not go down to take them away. Let him who is in the field likewise not turn back. Remember Lot's wife! Whoever seeks to save his life loses it, but whoever loses his life preserves it. I tell you, in that night there will be two people in one bed. The one will be taken, and the other will be left. There will be two grinding grain together. One will be taken, and the other will be left."*

They answering, asked him, "Where, Lord?"

He said to them, *"Where the body is, there will the vultures also be gathered together."*—[Luke 17:20-37]

THE PARABLE of the PERSISTENT WIDOW

He also spoke a parable to them that they must always pray, and not give up, saying, *"There was a judge in a certain city who didn't fear God, and didn't respect man. A widow was in that city, and she often came to him, saying, 'Defend me from my adversary!' He wouldn't for a while, but afterward he said to himself, 'Though I neither fear God, nor respect man, yet because this widow bothers me, I will defend her, or else she will wear me out by her continual coming.'"*

The Lord said, *"Listen to what the unrighteous judge says. Won't God avenge His chosen ones, who are crying out to Him day and night, and yet He exercises patience with them? I tell you that He will avenge them quickly. Nevertheless, when the Son of Man comes, will He find faith on the earth?"*—[Luke 18:1-8]

THE PHARISEE and the TAX COLLECTOR

He spoke also this parable to certain people who were convinced of their own righteousness, and who despised all others. *"Two men went up into the temple to pray; one was a Pharisee, and the other was a tax collector. The Pharisee stood and prayed to himself like this: 'God, I thank you, that I am not like the rest of men, extortioners, unrighteous, adulterers, or even like this tax collector. I fast twice a week. I give tithes of all that I get.' But the tax collector, standing far*

*away, wouldn't even lift up his eyes to heaven, but beat his breast,
saying, 'God, be merciful to me, a sinner!' I tell you, this man went
down to his house justified rather than the other; for everyone who
exalts himself will be humbled, but he who humbles himself will be
exalted."*—[Luke 18:9-14]

TEACHING ABOUT DIVORCE

When Jesus had finished saying these things, He left Galilee and went into
the region of Judea beyond the Jordan. Again crowds of people followed
Him, and as was His custom, He taught them and healed them there.

Some Pharisees came to Jesus to test His. They asked, "Is it lawful for a man
to divorce his wife for any and every reason?"

Jesus replied, *"What did Moses command you?"*

They said, "Moses permitted a man to write a certificate of divorce and
send her away."

*"It was because your hearts were hard that Moses wrote you this
law,"* Jesus replied. *"But it was not this way at the beginning of
creation. For God 'made them male and female. 'For this reason a
man will leave his father and mother and be united to his wife, and
the two will become one flesh.' So they are no longer two, but one
flesh. Therefore what God has joined together, let no one separate. I
tell you that anyone who divorces his wife, except for sexual
immorality, and marries another woman commits adultery."*

In the house, His disciples asked Him about this matter. He answered,
*"Anyone who divorces his wife and marries another woman commits
adultery against her. And if she divorces her husband and marries
another man, she commits adultery."*

Then, they said to Him, "If this is the situation between a husband and wife,
it is better not to marry."

Jesus replied, *"Not everyone can accept this word, but only those to whom it has been given. For there are eunuchs who were born that way, and there are eunuchs who have been made eunuchs by others—and there are those who choose to live like eunuchs for the sake of the kingdom of heaven. The one who can accept this should accept it."* —[Matthew 19:3-12 and Mark 10:2-12 *harmonized*]

People from the multitudes were bringing their babies to Jesus, little children, that He should lay His hands on them and pray; but His disciples rebuked them. When Jesus saw it, He was moved with indignation, and said to them, *"Allow the little children to come to me, and don't hinder them, for the Kingdom of God belongs to such as these. Most assuredly, I tell you, whoever doesn't receive the Kingdom of God like a little child, he will in no way enter into it."* He took them in his arms, and blessed them, laying His hands on them and departed from there. —[Matthew 19:13-15, Mark 10:13-16, and Luke 18:15-17]

THE RICH YOUNG MAN

As Jesus was setting out on a journey, a man ran up to Him and fell on his knees before Him. He asked, "Good Teacher, what must I do to inherit eternal life?"

"Why do you call me good?" Jesus answered. *"No one is good—except God alone. If you want to enter life, keep the commandments."*

"Which ones?" he inquired.

Jesus replied, *"You shall not murder, you shall not commit adultery, you shall not steal, you shall not give false testimony, honor your father and mother, and love your neighbor as yourself."*

"All these I have kept since I was a boy," the young man said. "What do I still lack?"

Jesus looked at him and loved him. *"One thing you lack,"* He said. *"If you want to be perfect, go, sell everything you have and give to the poor, and you will have treasure in heaven. Then come, follow me."*

When the young man heard this, he went away sad, because he had great wealth. Jesus looked around and said to His disciples, *"How hard it is for the rich to enter the kingdom of God!"*

The disciples were amazed at His words. But Jesus said again, *"Children, how hard it is to enter the kingdom of God! It is easier for a camel to go through the eye of a needle than for someone who is rich to enter the kingdom of God."*

The disciples were even more amazed, and said to each other, "Who then can be saved?"

Jesus looked at them and said, *"With man this is impossible, but not with God; all things are possible with God."*

Peter answered Him, "We have left everything to follow You! What then will there be for us?"

"Truly I tell you," Jesus replied, *"no one who has left home or brothers or sisters or mother or father or children or fields for me and the gospel will fail to receive a hundred times as much in this present age: homes, brothers, sisters, mothers, children and fields—with persecutions—and eternal life in the age to come. But many who are first will be last, and the last first."*—[Matthew 19:16-30, Mark 10:17-31, and Luke 18:18-30

PARABLE of the LABORERS IN THE VINEYARD

"For the Kingdom of Heaven is like a man who was the master of a household, who went out early in the morning to hire laborers for his vineyard. When he had agreed with the laborers for a denarius a day, he sent them into his vineyard. He went out about the third hour, and saw others standing idle in the marketplace. To them he said, 'You

*also go into the vineyard, and whatever is right I will give you.' So
they went their way. Again he went out about the <u>sixth and the ninth
hour,</u> and did likewise. About the <u>eleventh hour</u> he went out, and
found others standing idle. He said to them, 'Why do you stand here
all day idle?'*

"They said to him, 'Because no one has hired us.'

*"He said to them, 'You also go into the vineyard, and you will receive
whatever is right.' When evening had come, the lord of the vineyard
said to his steward, 'Call the laborers and pay them their wages,
beginning from the last to the first.'*

*"When those who were hired at about the eleventh hour came, they
each received a denarius. When the first came, they supposed that
they would receive more; and they likewise each received a denarius.
When they received it, they murmured against the master of the
household, saying, 'These last have spent one hour, and you have
made them equal to us, who have borne the burden of the day and the
scorching heat!'*

*"But he answered one of them, 'Friend, I am doing you no wrong.
Didn't you agree with me for a denarius? Take that which is yours,
and go your way. It is my desire to give to this last just as much as to
you. Isn't it lawful for me to do what I want to with what I own? Or is
your eye evil, because I am good?' So the last will be first, and the first
last. For many are called, but few are chosen."*—[Matthew 20:1-16]

<u>JESUS AGAIN PREDICTS HIS DEATH -3RD TIME</u>

Jesus was going up to Jerusalem, traveling in front of His disciples who
were in awe of Him, He took the twelve disciples aside, and on the way, told
them, *"See, we are going up to Jerusalem, and everything that is
written by the prophets about the Son of Man will be fulfilled. The Son
of Man will be delivered over to the chief priests and the teachers of
the law. They will condemn Him to death and will hand Him over to*

the Gentiles to be mocked, shamefully treated, spit upon, and flogged. After this He will be crucified. On the third day, He will rise again."

The disciples did not understand any of this. Its meaning was hidden from them, and they did not know what He was talking about.—[Matthew 20:17-19, Mark 10-32-34, Luke 18:31-34]

JAMES' & JOHN'S REQUEST

Then the mother of James and John (who were the sons of Zebedee), came to Jesus with her sons. Kneeling down, she asked a favor of Him. *"What is it you want?"* He asked.

She said, "Grant that one of these two sons of mine may sit at Your right and the other at your left in Your kingdom."

"You don't know what you are asking," Jesus said to them. *"Can you drink the cup I am going to drink or be baptized with the baptism I am baptized with?"*

"We can," they answered.

Jesus said to them, *"You will indeed drink from my cup and be baptized with the baptism I am baptized with, but to sit at my right or left is not for me to grant. These places belong to those for whom they have been prepared by my Father."*

When the ten heard about this, they became indignant with James and John. Jesus called them together and said, *"You know that the rulers of the Gentiles lord it over them, and their high officials exercise authority over them. Not so with you. Instead, whoever wants to become great among you must be your servant, and whoever wants to be first must be the slave of all—just as the Son of Man did not come to be served, but to serve, and to give His life as a ransom for many."*—[Matthew 20:20-28 and Mark 10:35-45]

CHAPTER 17

THE HEALING OF BLIND BARTIMAEUS

As they went out from Jericho, a great multitude followed Him. It happened, as he came near Jericho, a certain blind man sat by the road, begging. Hearing a multitude going by, he asked what this meant. They told him that Jesus of Nazareth was passing by. Behold, he was one of two blind men who sat by the road. When the blind men heard that Jesus was passing by, they each cried out, "Lord, have mercy on me, you son of David!" The multitude rebuked them, telling them that they should be quiet, but they cried out even more, "Lord, have mercy on us, you son of David!"

One of blind men was the son of Timaeus, and his name was Bartimaeus. He was a beggar.

Jesus, being moved with compassion, stood still, and said, *"Call him."* They called Bartimaeus, saying to him, "Cheer up! Get up. He is calling you!" Casting away his cloak, Bartameus sprang up and came to Jesus. The other blind man also came near Jesus and Jesus asked both of them *"What do you want me to do for you?"* They each replied saying they wished for their eyes to be opened (that sight might be restored).

He touched their eyes and said to them, *"Receive your sight and go your way. Your faith has made you well.";* and immediately Bartimaeus received his sight as did the other blind man. Bartameus, however, began glorifying God. Both men, having been profoundly changed, followed Jesus. All the people, when they saw it, praised God. —[Matthew 20:29-34, Mark 10:46-52, and Luke 18:35-43]

JESUS VISITS ZACCHAEUS

He entered and was passing through Jericho. There was a man named Zacchaeus. He was a chief tax collector, and he was rich. He was trying to see who Jesus was, and couldn't see over the crowd, because he was short. He ran on ahead, and climbed up into a sycamore tree to see Him, for He was to pass that way. When Jesus came to the place, He looked up and saw him, and said to him, ***"Zacchaeus, hurry and come down, for today I must stay at your house."*** He hurried, came down, and received Him joyfully. When they saw it, they all murmured, saying, "He has gone in to lodge with a man who is a sinner."

Zacchaeus stood and said to the Lord, "Behold, Lord, half of my goods I give to the poor. If I have wrongfully exacted anything of anyone, I restore four times as much."

Jesus said to him, ***"Today, salvation has come to this house, because he also is a son of Abraham. For the Son of Man came to seek and to save that which was lost."***—[Luke 19-1:10]

THE PARABLE OF THE TEN MINAS

As they heard these things, He went on and told a parable, because He was near Jerusalem, and they supposed that the Kingdom of God would be revealed immediately. He said therefore, ***"A certain nobleman went into a far country to receive for himself a kingdom, and to return. He called ten servants of his, and gave them ten mina coins, and told them, 'Conduct business until I come.' But his citizens hated him, and sent an envoy after him, saying, 'We don't want this man to reign over us.'***

"It happened when he had come back again, having received the kingdom, that he commanded these servants, to whom he had given the money, to be called to him, that he might know what they had gained by conducting business. The first came before him, saying, 'Lord, your mina has made ten more minas.'

"He said to him, 'Well done, you good servant! Because you were found faithful with very little, you shall have authority over ten cities.'

"The second came, saying, 'Your mina, Lord, has made five minas.'

"So he said to him, 'And you are to be over five cities.' Another came, saying, 'Lord, behold, your mina, which I kept laid away in a handkerchief, for I feared you, because you are an exacting man. You take up that which you didn't lay down, and reap that which you didn't sow.'

"He said to him, 'Out of your own mouth will I judge you, you wicked servant! You knew that I am an exacting man, taking up that which I didn't lay down, and reaping that which I didn't sow. Then why didn't you deposit my money in the bank, and at my coming, I might have earned interest on it?' He said to those who stood by, 'Take the mina away from him, and give it to him who has the ten minas.'

"They said to him, 'Lord, he already has ten minas!' 'For I tell you that to everyone who has, will more be given; but from him who doesn't have, even that which he has will be taken away from him. But bring those enemies of mine who didn't want me to reign over them here, and kill them before me.'"—[Luke 19:11-27]

JESUS ANOINTED at BETHANY

Now, it was six days before the Passover, and Jesus came to Bethany, where Lazarus lived, whom He had raised from the dead. He had been invited to Simon the Leper's house. This Simon was also a Pharisee and there was, at his house, a dinner in Jesus' honor. Martha served, while Lazarus was among those reclining at the table with Him.

As they were eating, a woman came with an alabaster jar containing a pound of very expensive perfume, made of pure nard. She was Mary, the sister of Martha and Lazarus, and she approached Jesus, from behind as he reclined at the table. Suddenly, she broke the alabaster jar, poured the perfume on His head and His feet while she wept. The house was filled with the fragrance of the perfume and as her tears fell upon His feet, Mary wiped them off with her hair.

When the disciples and others present saw this, they were indignant and said to one another, "Why this waste?" One of the disciples, Judas Iscariot, who would later betray Him, rebuked her harshly saying, "Why wasn't this perfume sold for three hundred denarii and the money given to the poor? It was worth a year's wages!" He did not say this because he cared about the poor but because he was a thief; as keeper of the money bag, he used to help himself to what was put into it.

But Jesus, aware of their thoughts, said, *"Leave her alone. Why are you bothering her? She has done a beautiful thing to me. The poor you will always have with you, but you will not always have me. She did what she could; she poured perfume on my body beforehand to prepare me for my burial. Truly I tell you, wherever this gospel is preached throughout the world, what she has done will also be told, in memory of her."*

As Simon, the Pharisee, watched, he said to himself, "If this man were a prophet, He would know who is touching Him and what kind of woman she is—that she is a sinner."

Jesus answered Him, *"Simon, I have something to tell you."*

"Tell me, teacher," he said.

"Two people owed money to a certain moneylender. One owed him five hundred denarii, and the other fifty. Neither of them had the money to pay him back, so he forgave the debts of both. Now which of them will love him more?"

Simon replied, "I suppose the one who had the bigger debt forgiven."

"You have judged correctly," Jesus said.

Then He turned toward the woman and said to Simon, *"Do you see this woman? I came into your house. You did not give me any water for my feet, but she wet my feet with her tears and wiped them with her hair. You did not give me a kiss, but this woman, from the time I entered, has not stopped kissing my feet. You did not put oil on my head, but she has poured perfume on my feet. Therefore, I tell you, her many sins have been forgiven—as her great love has shown. But whoever has been forgiven little loves little."*

Then Jesus said to her, **"Your sins are forgiven."**

The other guests began to say among themselves, "Who is this who even forgives sins?"

Jesus said to the woman, **"Your faith has saved you; go in peace."**—[Matthew 26:6-13, Mark 14:3-9, Luke 7:36-50, and John 12:1-8 *harmonized*

*Important note from the compiler:

<u>*Debate on Mary of Bethany and Mary Magdalene*</u>

There is debate among scholars concerning whether Mary Magdalene and Mary "of Bethany" were the same person. Some believe they were entirely distinct individuals. However, there is strong evidence in the Scriptures to suggest that Mary "of Bethany" and Mary "of Magdala" (a.k.a Mary Magdalene) are one and the same. We have added the "of Bethany" as a designation to distinguish her from other Marys.

Mary was a common name back then (as was the name "Simon"), but how many "Marys" were close enough to Jesus (relationship-wise) to break an alabaster jar, anoint His feet, weep over them sorrowfully, and kiss them (all from genuine tender love that came from knowing Him and experiencing His goodness)?

The alabaster jar was so expensive that it was said to be worth more than a year's wages and more than 300 denarii! It makes sense, therefore, to infer that Mary "of Bethany," who sat at Jesus's feet to hear His teaching and later witnessed Him raising her brother Lazarus from the dead, would have appreciated Jesus enough to sacrifice an alabaster jar in His honor. After all, that jar was significantly worth less in comparison to His goodness toward her family. If she were indeed Mary Magdalene, who Jesus had liberated from her bondage to seven demons, she would indeed appreciate Him all the more!

<u>*Wealth and Actions of Mary:*</u>

We can also infer that Mary of Bethany was wealthy since she owned such an expensive item in the first place! But why wouldn't she also have been at the foot of the cross as someone who clearly loved Jesus more than most (that is if we assume she was an entirely different woman from Mary Magdalene)? Or at the tomb after His resurrection? With that said, why can't Mary of Bethany and Mary Magdalene be one and the same? It's quite possible, quite likely, and I firmly believe it is the case!

Similarities between the Marys

- *Wealth*

  Mary Magdalene traveled with Jesus and helped support His ministry financially. If she were well-to-do, an alabaster jar might have been as affordable to her as Mary of Bethany (c.f. Luke 8:1-3).

- *Readiness to annoint Jesus*

  She, who was the first to go to the tomb to anoint the Lord's body, (according to Mark 16:1), could easily have been the same Mary "of Bethany" who had anointed Him a first time at Simon the Leper's house.

- *Sinfulness*

  Having had seven demons cast out of her would most certainly have implied she was once "a very sinful woman" (as demons do not live righteously and are anything but Holy). Interestingly enough, this lines up with Simon the leper's view of her when he said to Himself..."If this man were a prophet, He would know what kind of woman was touching Him...a very sinful woman." -Luke 7:39

Since Mary of Bethany broke the alabaster jar without hesitation to honor her Lord, He must have been worth more than her most precious possessions. It would stand to reason that she would financially support Jesus's ministry (as Mary Magdalene did). Moreover, if she felt such great honor in anointing Christ before His burial, why not after, as Mary

Magdalene had intended to do before learning that He had risen from the grave?

<u>Harmonizing Simon the Leper and Simon the Pharisee:</u>

As the compiler of these scriptures from the Gospels, I've chosen to refrain from long commentaries and from paraphrasing the accounts (for the most part). Neither have I sought the title of author for this particular project because my sincere goal (primarily) was to show the true harmony of the Gospel and that it is one seamless narrative (though recounted from four different perspectives captured in four distinct writing styles).

It is only through careful reading, adequate comprehension, and allowing the guidance of the Holy Spirit that we can eliminate all seeming contradictions. Additionally, I'd like to help spread the understanding that specific characters, especially those mentioned multiple times, deserve more scrutiny and investigation than we have previously given them. For instance, you've noticed that I identify Simon the Pharisee in the same breath as Simon the Leper. In two gospels, he is referred to as "Simon the leper" (Matthew 26 and Mark 14). In another, a Pharisee (Luke 7) whose name we deduce to be Simon and just as with Mary, many scholars believe Simon the Leper and Simon the Pharisee are different people. This is highly unlikely.

The three curiously similar accounts found in Matthew, Mark, and Luke illustrate the necessity for harmonizing the scriptures because it is extremely improbable that each time Jesus reclined at the dinner table of a man who happened to be named Simon, a woman who was not a hired servant anointed Him before the Passover, just to elicit the same reactions (respectively) from the host and some of His disciples. Stranger yet is the fact that none of the accounts acknowledge a dejavu. If I were among the four apostles who wrote gospels, I would've seen the black cat twice and said something.

Speculative Connections:

Finally (and this part is more speculative), it may be that Simon the Leper was a specific leper. Not just "a leper by the name of Simon" (emphasis on the indefinite article), but Simon "the" leper (definite article). You see, Jesus healed many, but there was one leper in particular whom He healed before healing the ten lepers he met with later on. That one was one of two who were given specific instructions on how to obtain (or possibly regain) purity "legally" by following the Mosaic tradition.

Unfortunately the second leper was a Samaritan (and he certainly would not have been accepted among the Pharisees). In an effort to harmonize the scriptures, I could not overlook the possibility of the first leper Jesus healed being "the leper" who invited Christ for dinner. Lepers technically could not be part of the community of Pharisees, except with one potential loophole.

We should note that generations earlier, God caused Moses' hand to momentarily become leprous at the burning bush (in Exodus 4:6-7), and made his sister Miriam leprous after speaking against Moses for marrying a Cushite woman (in Numbers 12:1-15). Even so, both were made clean again, and this did not affect their calling and/or status among the Israelites. Likewise, the healing may have allowed Simon to continue his life in the Pharisaical circle. Therefore, it may be that after "the" Leper obeyed Jesus' instructions to show himself to the priest and offer the gift that Moses commanded, for proof was the one who invited Christ to dine with Him. After all, how many Pharisees were inclined to sit with Christ seeing that He brought "sinners" with Him? Not many; but gratitude can be a strong motivator.

Is it not interesting that of all the healings that Jesus performed, He only had lepers show proof according to the Law? Could it have been because although the Pharisees were generally hypocritical in many ways, they were regarded as followers and keepers of "the Law." So, what if Simon the Leper was, in fact, the same one Jesus had healed earlier? A person could not be a Pharisee and a leper, but if he were completely healed and therefore clean according to the Law, could he be reinstated?

Finally, it could be that Jesus was directing His parable at Simon when He said "Simon, I have something to tell you" and then proceeded to compare the situation between the money lender who forgave the little debt and the big debt and what Simon had done for Him compared with Mary's display of gratitude. The one who is forgiven of a greater debt will love more. Once more, this connection between Simon the Leper (and Pharisee) and the leper healed earlier in Jesus' ministry is a sensible possibility that scripture neither denies nor confirms, it's just fun to consider.

End note.]

THE PLOT TO KILL LAZARUS

A large crowd of the Jews, therefore, learned that He was there, and they came, not for Jesus' sake only, but that they might see Lazarus also, whom He had raised from the dead. But the chief priests conspired to put Lazarus to death also, because on account of him many of the Jews went away and believed in Jesus.—[John 12:9-11]

CHAPTER 18

TRIUMPHAL ENTRY

On the next day a great multitude had come to the feast.

When Jesus and His disciples drew near to Jerusalem and Bethany, and came to Bethphage, to the mount called Olivet (or the Mount of Olives), He sent two disciples, saying to them, *"Go into the village that is opposite you, and immediately as you enter it, you will find a donkey tied, on which no one has sat, and a colt with her. Untie them, and bring them to me. If anyone says anything to you, you shall say, 'The Lord needs them,' and immediately He will send them back here."*

All this was done, that it might be fulfilled which was spoken through the prophet, saying,

"Tell the daughter of Zion,

 Behold, your King comes to you,

 Humble, and riding on a donkey,

 On a colt, the foal of a donkey."

The disciples went, and did just as Jesus commanded them, found a young donkey tied at the door outside in the open street, and they untied him. Some of those who stood there asked them, "What are you doing, untying the young donkey?" They said to them just as Jesus had said, and they let them go. The disciples brought the donkey and the colt, and laid their clothes on them; and Jesus sat on them. When the multitude in Jerusalem heard that Jesus was coming there, they took the branches of the palm trees, and went out to meet Him, and cried out, "Hosanna! Blessed is He who comes in the name of the Lord, the King of Israel!" They spread their clothes on the road. Others who had cut branches from the trees, spread the branches on the road. The multitudes who went before Him, and who followed kept shouting their praises, "Hosanna to the son of David! Blessed is the kingdom of our father David; the kingdom that is coming in the name of the Lord! Hosanna in the highest!"

As it is written, "Don't be afraid, daughter of Zion. Behold, your King comes, sitting on a donkey's colt." His disciples didn't understand these things at first, but when Jesus was glorified, then they remembered that these things were written about Him, and that they had done these things to Him. The multitude therefore that was with Him when he called Lazarus out of the tomb, and raised him from the dead, was testifying about it. For this cause also the multitude went and met Him, because they heard that He had done this sign. The Pharisees therefore said among themselves, "See how you accomplish nothing. Behold, the world has gone after Him."

When He had come into Jerusalem, all the city was stirred up, saying, "Who is this?" The multitudes said, "This is the prophet, Jesus, from Nazareth of Galilee."

Jesus entered into the temple in Jerusalem. When He had looked around at everything, as it was already late, He went out to Bethany with the twelve. —[Matthew 21:1-11, Mark 11:1-11, Luke 19:29-44, and John 12:12-19]

SOME GREEKS SEEK JESUS

Now there were certain Greeks among those that went up to worship at the feast. These, therefore, came to Philip, who was from Bethsaida of Galilee, and asked him, saying, "Sir, we want to see Jesus." Philip came and told Andrew, and in turn, Andrew came with Philip, and they told Jesus. Jesus answered them, *"The time has come for the Son of Man to be glorified. Most assuredly I tell you, unless a grain of wheat falls into the earth and dies, it remains by itself alone. But if it dies, it bears much fruit. He who loves his life will lose it. He who hates his life in this world will keep it to eternal life. If anyone serves me, let him follow me. Where I am, there will my servant also be. If anyone serves me, the Father will honor him.*—[John 12:20-26]

THE SON of MAN MUST BE LIFTED UP

"Now my soul is troubled. What shall I say? 'Father, save me from this time?' But for this cause I came to this hour. Father, glorify Your name!"

Then there came a voice out of the sky, saying, "I have both glorified it, and will glorify it again."

The multitude therefore, who stood by and heard it, said that it had thundered. Others said, "An angel has spoken to Him."

Jesus answered, *"This voice hasn't come for my sake, but for your sakes. Now is the judgment of this world. Now the prince of this world will be cast out. And I, if I am lifted up from the earth, will draw all people to myself."* But He said this, signifying by what kind of death He should die. The multitude answered Him, "We have heard out of the law that the Christ remains forever. How do You say, *'The Son of Man must be lifted up?' Who is this Son of Man?"*

Jesus therefore said to them, "Yet a little while the light is with you. Walk while you have the light, that darkness doesn't overtake you. He who walks in the darkness doesn't know where he is going. While you have the light, believe in the light, that you may become children of light."—[John 12:27-36]

SPIRITUAL BLINDNESS & LACK of FAITH

Jesus said these things, and He departed and hid Himself from them. But though He had done so many signs before them, yet they didn't believe in Him, that the word of Isaiah the prophet might be fulfilled, which he spoke,

"Lord, who has believed our report?
    To whom has the arm of the Lord been revealed?"

For this cause they couldn't believe, for Isaiah said again,

"He has blinded their eyes and He hardened their heart,
    Lest they should see with their eyes,
    And perceive with their heart,

And would turn,
And I would heal them."

Isaiah said these things when he saw His glory, and spoke of Him. Nevertheless even of the rulers many believed in Him, but because of the Pharisees they didn't confess it, so that they wouldn't be put out of the synagogue, for they loved men's praise more than God's praise.—[John 12:36-43]

JESUS REPRESENTS the FATHER

Jesus cried out and said, *"Whoever believes in me, believes not in me, but in Him who sent me. He who sees me sees Him who sent me. I have come as a light into the world, that whoever believes in me may not remain in the darkness. If anyone listens to my sayings, and doesn't believe, I don't judge him. For I came not to judge the world, but to save the world. He who rejects me, and doesn't receive my sayings, has one who judges him. The word that I spoke, the same will judge him in the last day. For I spoke not from myself, but the Father who sent me, He gave me a commandment, what I should say, and what I should speak. I know that His commandment is eternal life. The things therefore which I speak, even as the Father has said to me, so I speak.*—[John 12:44-50]

CURSING THE FIG TREE

The next day as Jesus was leaving Bethany on His way back to Jerusalem, He was hungry. Seeing, in the distance, a fig tree by the road in leaf, He went to find out if it had any fruit. When He reached it, He found nothing but leaves, because it was not the season for figs. Then He said to the tree, "May no one ever eat fruit from you again." And His disciples heard Him say it.

The fig tree withered at once from the roots. —[Matthew 21:18-19 and Mark 11:12-14 *harmonized*]

JESUS CLEANSES THE TEMPLE

~The moment Jesus entered the temple courts, a righteous anger was ignited within Him. Seeing signs of mammon in a place that was supposed to be sacred,~He began driving out those who were buying and selling there. He overturned the tables of the money changers and the benches of those selling doves. He would not allow anyone to carry merchandise through the temple courts.

He taught them, *"Is it not written: 'My house will be called a house of prayer for all nations'? But you have made it 'a den of robbers.'"*

The chief priests and the teachers of the law heard this and began looking for a way to kill Him, for they feared Him because the whole crowd was amazed at His teaching. But they could not find any way to do it, because all the people hung on His words.

The blind and the lame came to Him at the temple, and He healed them. But when the chief priests and the teachers of the law saw the wonderful things He did and the children shouting in the temple courts, "Hosanna to the Son of David," they were indignant.

"Do you hear what these children are saying?" they asked Him.

"Yes," replied Jesus, *"have you never read, 'From the lips of children and infants You, Lord, have called forth Your praise'?"*

And He left them and went out of the city to Bethany, where He spent the night.—[Matthew 21:12-17, Mark 11:15-19, and Luke 19:45-48] Note: Luke says "He was teaching daily there…"

THE LESSON BEHIND THE WITHERED FIG TREE

In the following morning, on the way back to Jerusalem, they saw the fig tree had withered away. Peter, remembering Jesus' words, said to Him,

"Rabbi, look! The fig tree You cursed has withered!" When the disciples saw it they marveled saying, "How did the fig tree wither at once?

Jesus replied, *"Have faith in God. Truly I tell you, if you have faith and do not doubt, not only can you do what was done to the fig tree, but also you can say to this mountain, 'Go, throw yourself into the sea,' and it will be done. If you believe, you will receive whatever you ask for in prayer."*

And when you stand praying, if you hold anything against anyone, forgive them, so that your Father in heaven may forgive you your sins.—[Matthew 21:20-22 and Mark 11:20-26]

CHALLENGING THE AUTHORITY OF JESUS

When He had returned into the temple (in Jerusalem), the chief priests, scribes, and the elders of the people came to Him as He was teaching and preaching the Gospel, and began questioning Him saying, "By what authority do You do these things? Who gave You this authority?"

Jesus answered them, *"I also will ask you one question, which if you tell me, I likewise will tell you by what authority I do these things. The baptism of John, where was it from? From heaven or from men? Answer me."*

They reasoned with themselves, saying, "If we say, 'From heaven,' He will ask us, 'Why then did you not believe him?' But if we say, 'From men,' we fear the multitude, that they will stone us, for all are persuaded in holding John as a prophet." They answered Jesus, and said, "We don't know."

Jesus said to them, *"Neither will I tell you by what authority I do these things."*—[Matthew 21:23-27, Mark 11:27-33, and Luke 20:1-8] *...But what do you think? A man had two sons, and he came to the first, and said, 'Son, go work today in my vineyard.' He answered, 'I will not,' but afterward he changed his mind, and went. He came to the second, and said the same thing. He answered, 'I go, sir,' but he didn't go. Which of the two did the will of his father?"*

They said to Him, "The first."

Jesus said to them, *"Most assuredly I tell you that the tax collectors and the prostitutes are entering into the Kingdom of God before you. For John came to you in the way of righteousness, and you didn't believe him, but the tax collectors and the prostitutes believed him. When you saw it, you didn't even repent afterward, that you might believe him.*—[Matthew 21:28-32]

PARABLE OF THE WICKED TENANTS

He began to speak to them in parables. *"Hear another parable."* He continued, *"There was a man who was a master of a household, who planted a vineyard, set a hedge about it, dug a pit for a winepress, built a tower, leased it out to farmers, and went into another country. When the season for the fruit drew near, he sent a servant to the farmers to receive his share of the fruit. They beat him and sent him away empty. He sent more of his servants to the farmers, who took his servants, beat one, killed another, and stoned another. Again, he sent other servants more than the first: and they treated them the same way. But afterward he sent to them his son, saying, 'They will respect my son.' But the farmers, when they saw the son, said among themselves, 'This is the heir. Come, let's kill him, and seize his inheritance.' So they took him, and threw him out of the vineyard, and killed him. When therefore the lord of the vineyard comes, what will he do to those farmers?"*

They told Him, "He will miserably destroy those men, and will lease out the vineyard to other farmers, who will give Him the fruit in its season."

"He will come and destroy these farmers, won't He? And will give the vineyard to others."

When they heard it, they said, "May it never be!"

Jesus replied, *"Did you never read in the Scriptures,*

'The stone which the builders rejected,

The same was made the chief cornerstone; the head of the corner.

This was from the Lord.

It is marvelous in our eyes?'

"Therefore I tell you, the Kingdom of God will be taken away from you, and will be given to a nation bringing forth its fruits. He who falls on this stone will be broken to pieces, but on whoever it will fall, it will scatter him as dust."

When the chief priests and the Pharisees heard His parables, they perceived that He spoke about them. When they sought to seize Him that very hour, they feared the multitudes, because they considered Him to be a prophet.—[Matthew 21:33-46, Mark 12:1-12, Luke 20:9-18]

THE PARABLE OF the WEDDING FEAST

Jesus answered and spoke again in parables to them, saying, *"The Kingdom of Heaven is like a certain king, who made a marriage feast for his son, and sent out his servants to call those who were invited to the marriage feast, but they would not come. Again he sent out other servants, saying, 'Tell those who are invited, "Behold, I have made ready my dinner. My oxen and my fatlings are killed, and all things are ready. Come to the marriage feast!"' But they made light of it, and went their ways, one to his own farm, another to his merchandise, and the rest grabbed his servants, and treated them shamefully, and killed them. When the king heard that, he was angry, and he sent his armies, destroyed those murderers, and burned their city.*

"Then he said to his servants, 'The wedding is ready, but those who were invited weren't worthy. Go therefore to the intersections of the highways, and as many as you may find, invite to the marriage feast.' Those servants went out into the highways, and gathered together as many as they found, both bad and good. The wedding was filled with

guests. But when the king came in to see the guests, he saw there a man who didn't have on wedding clothing, and he said to him, 'Friend, how did you come in here not wearing wedding clothing?' He was speechless. Then the king said to the servants, 'Bind him hand and foot, take him away, and throw him into the outer darkness; there is where the weeping and grinding of teeth will be.' For many are called, but few chosen."—[Matthew 22:1-14]

PAYING TAXES TO CAESAR

They left Him, and went away. They sent some of the Pharisees and of the Herodians to Him as spies who pretended to be righteous, that they might trap Him with words, so as to deliver Him up to the power and authority of the governor. When they had come, they asked Him, "Teacher, we know that You are honest, and don't defer to anyone; for You aren't partial to anyone, but truly teach the way of God. Is it lawful to pay taxes to Caesar, or not? Shall we give, or shall we not give?" But He perceived their craftiness, and said to them, ***"Why do you test me? Show me a denarius. Whose image and inscription are on it?"***

They answered, "Caesar's."

He said to them, ***"Then give to Caesar the things that are Caesar's, and to God the things that are God's."***

They weren't able to trap Him in His words before the people. They marveled at His answer, and were silent.—[Matthew 22:15-22, Mark 12:13-17, Luke 20:19-28]

RESURRECTION QUESTION FROM SADDUCEES

Some of the Sadducees, those who would say there is no resurrection, came to Jesus with a question. "Teacher," they said, "Moses wrote for us that if a man's brother dies and leaves a wife but no children, the man must marry the widow and raise up offspring for his brother. Now there were seven brothers. The first one married a woman and died childless. The second and then the third married her, and in the same way the seven died, leaving no children. Finally, the woman died too. Now then, at the resurrection, whose wife will she be, since the seven were married to her?"

Jesus replied, "Are you not in error because you do not know the Scriptures or the power of God? The people of this age marry and are given in marriage. But at the resurrection, people will neither marry nor be given in marriage; they will be like the angels in heaven. But about the resurrection of the dead—have you not read in the Book of Moses, in the account of the burning bush, how God said to him, 'I am the God of Abraham, the God of Isaac, and the God of Jacob'? He is not the God of the dead, but of the living. You are badly mistaken!"

Some of the teachers of the law responded, "Well said, Teacher!" And no one dared to ask him any more questions.—[Matthew 22:23-33, Mark 12:18-27, Luke 20:27-40]

THE GREATEST COMMANDMENT

Hearing that Jesus had silenced the Sadducees, the Pharisees joined forces. One of the teachers of the law, who was an expert in it, came and heard them debating. Noticing that Jesus had given them a good answer, he asked Him, "Teacher, which is the greatest commandment in the Law?"

Jesus replied, *"The most important one is this: 'Hear, O Israel: The Lord our God, the Lord is one. Love the Lord your God with all your heart and with all your soul and with all your mind and with all your strength.' This is the first and greatest commandment. And the second is like it: 'Love your neighbor as yourself.' There is no commandment greater than these. All the Law and the Prophets hang on these two commandments."*

"Well said, Teacher," the man replied. "You are right in saying that God is one and there is no other but Him. To love Him with all your heart, with all your understanding and with all your strength, and to love your neighbor as yourself is more important than all burnt offerings and sacrifices."

When Jesus saw that the teacher of law had answered wisely, He said to him, *"You are not far from the kingdom of God."* And from then on, no one dared ask Him any more questions.—[Matthew 22:34-40 and Mark 12:28-34]

WHOSE SON IS THE MESSIAH?

Now while the Pharisees were gathered together, Jesus who was still teaching at the temple asked them a question, saying, *"What do you think of the Christ? Whose son is He?"*

They said to Him, "Of David."

He said to them, *"How is it that the scribes say that the Christ is the son of David? For David himself—in the Book of Psalms—said in the Holy Spirit,*

'The Lord said to my Lord,

Sit on my right hand,

Until I make Your enemies a footstool for Your feet?'

"If then David calls him Lord, how is He his son?"

No one was able to answer Him a word, neither dared any man from that day forth ask Him any more questions and the common people heard Him gladly.—[Matthew 22:41-46, Mark 12:35-37, and Luke 20:41-44]

SEVEN WOES TO THE SCRIBES AND PHARISEES

Then Jesus said to the crowds and to His disciples: *"The teachers of the law and the Pharisees sit in Moses' seat. So you must be careful to do everything they tell you. But do not do what they do, for they do not practice what they preach. They tie up heavy, cumbersome loads and put them on other people's shoulders, but they themselves are not willing to lift a finger to move them.*

"Everything they do is done for people to see: They make their phylacteries wide and the tassels on their garments long; they love the place of honor at banquets and the most important seats in the synagogues; they love to be greeted with respect in the marketplaces and to be called 'Rabbi' by others.

"But you are not to be called 'Rabbi,' for you have one Teacher, and you are all brothers. And do not call anyone on earth 'father,' for you have one Father, and He is in heaven. Nor are you to be called instructors, for you have one Instructor, the Messiah. The greatest among you will be your servant. For those who exalt themselves will be humbled, and those who humble themselves will be exalted.

"Woe to you, teachers of the law and Pharisees, you hypocrites! You shut the door of the kingdom of heaven in people's faces. You yourselves do not enter, nor will you let those enter who are trying to.

"Woe to you, teachers of the law and Pharisees, you hypocrites! You travel over land and sea to win a single convert, and when you have succeeded, you make them twice as much a child of hell as you are.

"Woe to you, blind guides! You say, 'If anyone swears by the temple, it means nothing; but anyone who swears by the gold of the temple is bound by that oath.' You blind fools! Which is greater: the gold, or the temple that makes the gold sacred? You also say, 'If anyone swears by the altar, it means nothing; but anyone who swears by the gift on the altar is bound by that oath.' You blind men! Which is greater: the gift, or the altar that makes the gift sacred? Therefore, anyone who swears by the altar swears by it and by everything on it. And anyone who swears by the temple swears by it and by the one who dwells in it. And anyone who swears by heaven swears by God's throne and by the one who sits on it.

"Woe to you, teachers of the law and Pharisees, you hypocrites! You give a tenth of your spices—mint, dill and cumin. But you have neglected the more important matters of the law—justice, mercy and faithfulness. You should have practiced the latter, without neglecting

the former. You blind guides! You strain out a gnat but swallow a camel.

"Woe to you, teachers of the law and Pharisees, you hypocrites! You clean the outside of the cup and dish, but inside they are full of greed and self-indulgence. Blind Pharisee! First clean the inside of the cup and dish, and then the outside also will be clean.

"Woe to you, teachers of the law and Pharisees, you hypocrites! You are like whitewashed tombs, which look beautiful on the outside but on the inside are full of the bones of the dead and everything unclean. In the same way, on the outside you appear to people as righteous but on the inside you are full of hypocrisy and wickedness.

"Woe to you, teachers of the law and Pharisees, you hypocrites! You build tombs for the prophets and decorate the graves of the righteous. And you say, 'If we had lived in the days of our ancestors, we would not have taken part with them in shedding the blood of the prophets.' So you testify against yourselves that you are the descendants of those who murdered the prophets. Go ahead, then, and complete what your ancestors started!

"You snakes! You brood of vipers! How will you escape being condemned to hell? Therefore I am sending you prophets and sages and teachers. Some of them you will kill and crucify; others you will flog in your synagogues and pursue from town to town. And so upon you will come all the righteous blood that has been shed on earth, from the blood of righteous Abel to the blood of Zechariah son of Berekiah, whom you murdered between the temple and the altar. Truly I tell you, all this will come on this generation.

Jesus continued teaching, saying, *"Watch out for the teachers of the law. They like to walk around in flowing robes and love to be greeted with respect in the marketplaces and have the most important seats in the synagogues and the places of honor at banquets. They devour widows' houses and for a show make lengthy prayers. These men will be punished most severely."*—[Matthew 23:1-36, Mark 12:38-40, Luke 20:45-47]

LAMENT OVER JERUSALEM

"Jerusalem, Jerusalem, who kills the prophets and stones those who are sent to her! How often I would have gathered your children together, even as a hen gathers her chicks under her wings, and you would not! Behold, your house is left to you desolate. For I tell you, you will not see me from now on, until you say, 'Blessed is he who comes in the name of the Lord!' "—[Matthew 23:37-39]*

CHAPTER 19

THE WIDOW'S OFFERING

Jesus sat down opposite the place where the offerings were put and watched the crowd putting their money into the temple treasury. Many rich people threw in large amounts. But He also saw a poor widow come and put in two very small copper coins, worth only a few cents.

Calling His disciples to Him, Jesus said, *"Truly I tell you, this poor widow has put more into the treasury than all the others. All these people gave their gifts out of their wealth; but she, out of her poverty, put in everything—all she had to live on."*—[Mark 12:41-44, Luke 21:1-4]

SIGNS of the END TIMES

As Jesus was leaving the temple, one of His disciples said to Him, "Look, Teacher! What massive stones! What magnificent buildings!"

Jesus replied, *"Do you see all these great buildings? Not one stone here will be left on another; every one of them will be thrown down."*

Later, as Jesus was sitting on the Mount of Olives opposite the temple, Peter, James, John, and Andrew asked Him privately, "Tell us, when will these things happen? And what will be the sign that they are all about to be fulfilled?"

Jesus answered, *"Watch out that no one deceives you. For many will come in my name, claiming, 'I am the Messiah,' and will deceive many. You will hear of wars and rumors of wars, but see to it that you are not alarmed. Such things must happen, but the end is still to come. Nation will rise against nation, and kingdom against kingdom. There will be famines and earthquakes in various places. These are only the beginning of birth pains.*

"Be on your guard. You will be handed over to the local councils and flogged in the synagogues. On account of me, you will stand before governors and kings as witnesses to them. And the gospel must first be

preached to all nations. Whenever you are arrested and brought to trial, do not worry beforehand about what to say. Just say whatever is given you at the time, for it is not you speaking, but the Holy Spirit.

"Brother will betray brother to death, and a father his child. Children will rebel against their parents and have them put to death. Everyone will hate you because of me, but the one who stands firm to the end will be saved.

"When you see 'the abomination that causes desolation' standing where it does not belong (that is in the Holy place)—let the reader understand—then let those who are in Judea flee to the mountains. Let no one on the housetop go down to take anything out of the house. Let no one in the field go back to get their cloak. How dreadful it will be in those days for pregnant women and nursing mothers! Pray that this will not take place in winter or on the Sabbath, because those will be days of distress unequaled from the beginning, when God created the world, until now—and never to be equaled again.

"If those days had not been cut short, no one would survive, but for the sake of the elect those days will be shortened. At that time if anyone says to you, 'Look, here is the Messiah!' or, 'There He is!' do not believe it. For false messiahs and false prophets will appear and perform signs and wonders to deceive, if possible, even the elect. So be on your guard; I have told you everything ahead of time.

"So if anyone tells you, 'There He is, out in the wilderness,' do not go out; or, 'Here He is, in the inner rooms,' do not believe it. For as lightning that comes from the east is visible even in the west, so will be the coming of the Son of Man. Wherever there is a carcass, there the vultures will gather.

"Immediately after the distress of those days "'the sun will be darkened, and the moon will not give its light; the stars will fall from the sky, and the heavenly bodies will be shaken.'

"At that time people will see the Son of Man coming in clouds with great power and glory. And He will send His angels with a loud trumpet call, and they will gather His elect from the four winds, from the ends of the earth to the ends of the heavens.

"Now learn this lesson from the fig tree: As soon as its twigs get tender and its leaves come out, you know that summer is near. Even so, when you see these things happening, you know that it is near, right at the door. Truly I tell you, this generation will certainly not pass away until all these things have happened. Heaven and earth will pass away, but my words will never pass away.

"But about that day or hour no one knows, not even the angels in heaven, nor the Son, but only the Father. Be on guard! Be alert! You do not know when that time will come. It's like a man going away: He leaves his house and puts his servants in charge, each with their assigned task, and tells the one at the door to keep watch.

"Therefore keep watch, because you do not know on what day your Lord will come. But understand this: If the owner of the house had known at what time of night the thief was coming, he would have kept watch and would not have let his house be broken into. So you also must be ready, because the Son of Man will come at an hour when you do not expect Him.

"Who then is the faithful and wise servant, whom the master has put in charge of the servants in his household to give them their food at the proper time? It will be good for that servant whose master finds him doing so when he returns. Truly I tell you, he will put him in charge of all his possessions. But suppose that servant is wicked and says to himself, 'My master is staying away a long time,' and he then begins to beat his fellow servants and to eat and drink with drunkards. The master of that servant will come on a day when he does not expect him and at an hour he is not aware of. He will cut him to pieces and assign him a place with the hypocrites, where there will be weeping and gnashing of teeth.

"Be always on the watch, and pray that you may be able to escape all that is about to happen, and that you may be able to stand before the Son of Man."—[Matthew 24:1-51, Mark 13:1-37, and Luke 21:5-36]

PARABLE OF THE TEN VIRGINS

"Then the Kingdom of Heaven will be like ten virgins, who took their lamps, and went out to meet the bridegroom. Five of them were foolish, and five were wise. Those who were foolish, when they took their lamps, took no oil with them, but the wise took oil in their vessels with their lamps. Now while the bridegroom delayed, they all slumbered and slept. But at midnight there was a cry, 'Behold! The bridegroom is coming! Come out to meet him!' Then all those virgins arose, and trimmed their lamps. The foolish said to the wise, 'Give us some of your oil, for our lamps are going out.' But the wise answered, saying, 'What if there isn't enough for us and you? You go rather to those who sell, and buy for yourselves.' While they went away to buy, the bridegroom came, and those who were ready went in with him to the marriage feast, and the door was shut. Afterward the other virgins also came, saying, 'Lord, Lord, open to us.' But he answered, 'Most assuredly I tell you, I don't know you.' Watch therefore, for you don't know the day nor the hour in which the Son of Man is coming.—[Matthew 25:1-13]

PARABLE of the TALENTS

"For it is like a man, going into another country, who called his own servants, and entrusted his goods to them. To one he gave five talents, to another two, to another one; to each according to his own ability. Then he went on his journey. Immediately he who received the five talents went and traded with them, and made another five talents. In like manner he also who got the two gained another two. But he who received the one went away and dug in the earth, and hid his lord's money.

"Now after a long time the lord of those servants came, and reconciled accounts with them. He who received the five talents came and brought another five talents, saying, 'Lord, you delivered to me five talents. Behold, I have gained another five talents besides them.'

"His lord said to him, 'Well done, good and faithful servant. You have been faithful over a few things, I will set you over many things. Enter into the joy of your lord.'

"He also who got the two talents came and said, 'Lord, you delivered to me two talents. Behold, I have gained another two talents besides them.'

"His lord said to him, 'Well done, good and faithful servant. You have been faithful over a few things, I will set you over many things. Enter into the joy of your lord.'

"He also who had received the one talent came and said, 'Lord, I knew you that you are a hard man, reaping where you did not sow, and gathering where you did not scatter. I was afraid, and went away and hid your talent in the earth. Behold, you have what is yours.'

"But his lord answered him, 'You wicked and slothful servant. You knew that I reap where I didn't sow, and gather where I didn't scatter. You ought therefore to have deposited my money with the bankers, and at my coming I should have received back my own with interest. Take away therefore the talent from him, and give it to him who has the ten talents. For to everyone who has will be given, and he will have abundance, but from him who has not, even that which he has will be taken away. Throw out the unprofitable servant into the outer darkness, where there will be weeping and gnashing of teeth.'—[Matthew 25:14-30]

THE FINAL JUDGMENT

"But when the Son of Man comes in His glory, and all the holy angels with Him, then He will sit on the throne of His glory. Before Him all the nations will be gathered, and He will separate them one from another, as a shepherd separates the sheep from the goats. He will set the sheep on His right hand, but the goats on the left. Then the King will tell those on His right hand, 'Come, blessed of my Father, inherit the Kingdom prepared for you from the foundation of the world; for I was

hungry, and you gave me food to eat; I was thirsty, and you gave me drink; I was a stranger, and you took me in; naked, and you clothed me; I was sick, and you visited me; I was in prison, and you came to me.'

"Then the righteous will answer Him, saying, 'Lord, when did we see You hungry, and feed You; or thirsty, and give You a drink? When did we see You as a stranger, and take You in; or naked, and clothe You? When did we see You sick, or in prison, and come to You?'

"The King will answer them, 'Most assuredly I tell you, inasmuch as you did it to one of the least of these my brothers, you did it to me.' Then He will say also to those on the left hand, 'Depart from me, you cursed, into the eternal fire which is prepared for the devil and his angels; for I was hungry, and you didn't give me food to eat; I was thirsty, and you gave me no drink; was a stranger, and you didn't take me in; naked, and you didn't clothe me; sick, and in prison, and you didn't visit me.'

"Then they will also answer, saying, 'Lord, when did we see You hungry, or thirsty, or a stranger, or naked, or sick, or in prison, and didn't help You?'

"Then He will answer them, saying, 'Most assuredly I tell you, inasmuch as you didn't do it to one of the least of these, you didn't do it to me.' These will go away into eternal punishment, but the righteous into eternal life. "—[Matthew 25:31-46]

THE PLOT TO KILL JESUS

When Jesus had finished saying all these things, He said to His disciples, *"As you know, the Passover is two days away—and the Son of Man will be handed over to be crucified."*

Now the Passover and the Festival of Unleavened Bread were only two days away, and the chief priests, elders, and the teachers of the law were looking for a cunning way to arrest Jesus and kill Him. They assembled in the palace of the high priest, whose name was Caiaphas. And they secretly plotted, but said "Not during the festival, or there may be a riot among the people." —Matthew 26:1-5, Mark 14:1-2, and Luke 22:1-2]

CHAPTER 20

JUDAS AGREES to BETRAY JESUS

Satan entered into Judas, who was surnamed Iscariot, who was numbered with the twelve. He went to the chief priests and captains, and said, "What are you willing to give me, that I should deliver Him to you?" They, when they heard it, were glad, and promised tot give him money and weighed out for him thirty pieces of silver. From that time he sought a convenient opportunity to betray Him in the absence of the multitude. —[Matthew 26:14-16, Mark 14:10-11, and Luke 22:3-6]

THE LAST SUPPER

When evening came, Jesus was reclining at the table with the Twelve. The hour had come, and Jesus said to them, *"I have eagerly desired to eat this Passover with you before I suffer. For I tell you, I will not eat it again until it is fulfilled in the kingdom of God."* [Luke 22:14-16]

A dispute also arose among them as to which of them was considered to be greatest. Jesus said to them, *"The kings of the Gentiles lord it over them; and those who exercise authority over them call themselves Benefactors. But you are not to be like that. Instead, the greatest among you should be like the youngest, and the one who rules like the one who serves. For who is greater, the one who is at the table or the one who serves? Is it not the one who is at the table? But I am among you as one who serves.* [Luke 22:24-27]

Then Jesus said to them, *"When I sent you out with no moneybag or knapsack or sandals, did you lack anything?" They said, "Nothing." He said to them, "But now let the one who has a moneybag take it, and likewise a knapsack. And let the one who has no sword sell his cloak and buy one. For I tell you that this Scripture must be fulfilled in Me: 'And He was numbered with the transgressors.' For what is written about Me has its fulfillment" (Luke 22:35-37)."*

Jesus knew that the Father had put all things under His power, and that He had come from God and was returning to God; so He got up from the meal, took off His outer clothing, and wrapped a towel around His waist. After that, He poured water into a basin and began to wash His disciples' feet, drying them with the towel that was wrapped around Him. He came to Simon Peter, who said to Him, "Lord, are You going to wash my feet?" Jesus replied, *"You do not realize now what I am doing, but later you will understand."* "No," said Peter, "You shall never wash my feet." Jesus answered, *"Unless I wash you, you have no part with me."* "Then, Lord," Simon Peter replied, "not just my feet but my hands and my head as well!" Jesus answered, *"Those who have had a bath need only to wash their feet; their whole body is clean. And you are clean, though not every one of you."* For He knew who was going to betray Him, and that was why He said not everyone was clean. When He had finished washing their feet, He put on His clothes and returned to His place. *"Do you understand what I have done for you?" He asked them. "You call me 'Teacher' and 'Lord,' and rightly so, for that is what I am. Now that I, your Lord and Teacher, have washed your feet, you also should wash one another's feet. I have set you an example that you should do as I have done for you. Very truly I tell you, no servant is greater than his master, nor is a messenger greater than the one who sent him. Now that you know these things, you will be blessed if you do them."*

While they were eating, Jesus said, *"Truly I tell you, one of you will betray me."* They were very sad and began to say to Him one after the other, *"Surely you don't mean me, Lord?"* Jesus was troubled in spirit and testified, *"Very truly I tell you, one of you is going to betray me."*

His disciples stared at one another, at a loss to know which of them He meant. They began to question among themselves which of them it might be who would do this. Peter motioned to John, the beloved of Jesus to ask Jesus who He was referring to when He mentioned that one of them would betray Him. Jesus replied, *"The one who has dipped his hand into the bowl with me will betray me. "It is the one to whom I will give this piece of bread when I have dipped it in the dish. The Son of Man will go just as it is written about Him. But woe to that man who betrays the Son of Man! It would be better for him if he had not been born."* Then

Judas, the one who would betray Him, said, "Surely you don't mean me, Rabbi?" Jesus answered, ***"You have said so."***—(a common Jewish idiom that affirmed a statement made by another)

Then, dipping the piece of bread, he gave it to Judas, the son of Simon Iscariot. As soon as Judas took the bread, Satan entered into him.

So Jesus told him, ***"What you are about to do, do quickly."*** But no one else at the meal understood why Jesus said this to him. Since Judas had charge of the money, some thought Jesus was telling him to buy what was needed for the festival, or to give something to the poor. As soon as Judas had taken the bread, he went out. And it was night.

When he was gone, Jesus said, "Now the Son of Man is glorified and God is glorified in Him. If God is glorified in Him, God will glorify the Son in Himself, and will glorify Him at once."

While they were eating, Jesus took bread, and when He had given thanks, broke it and gave it to His disciples, saying, "Take and eat; this is my body." Then He took a cup, and when He had given thanks, He gave it to them, saying, "Drink from it, all of you. This is my blood of the covenant, which is poured out for many for the forgiveness of sins."

"I tell you, I will not drink from this fruit of the vine from now on until that day when I drink it again with you in my Father's kingdom." When they had sung a hymn, they went out to the Mount of Olives.

After they had sung a hymn and gone out to the Mount of Olives, Jesus said to them, "This very night you will all fall away on account of me, for it is written: 'I will strike the shepherd, and the sheep of the flock will be scattered.' But after I have risen, I will go ahead of you into Galilee."

Simon Peter answered Him, "Lord, where are You going?" Jesus replied, "Where I am going, you cannot follow now, but you will follow later." Peter asked, "Lord, why can't I follow You now? I will lay down my life for You."

Then Jesus told them, "Simon, Simon, Satan has asked to sift all of you as wheat. But I have prayed for you, Simon, that your faith may not fail. And when you have turned back, strengthen your brothers." But Peter replied,

"Even if all fall away on account of You, I never will. I am ready to go with You to prison and to death." Jesus answered, "Will you really lay down your life for me? Truly I tell you, this very night, before the rooster crows, you will disown me three times."

But Peter insisted emphatically, "Even if I have to die with You, I will never disown You." And all the other disciples said the same.—[Matthew 26:17-30, Mark 14:12-31, Luke 22:7-34, John 13:1-38]

THE WAY, THE TRUTH, and THE LIFE

"Don't let your heart be troubled. Believe in God. Believe also in me. In my Father's house are many mansions. If it weren't so, I would have told you. I am going to prepare a place for you. If I go and prepare a place for you, I will come again, and will receive you to myself; that where I am, you may be there also. Where I go, you know, and you know the way."

Thomas said to Him, "Lord, we don't know where You are going. How can we know the way?"

Jesus said to him, *"I am the way, the truth, and the life. No one comes to the Father, except through me. If you had known me, you would have known my Father also. From now on, you know Him, and have seen Him."*

Philip said to Him, "Lord, show us the Father, and that will be enough for us."

Jesus said to him, *"Have I been with you such a long time, and do you not know me, Philip? He who has seen me has seen the Father. How do you say, 'Show us the Father?' Don't you believe that I am in the Father, and the Father in me? The words that I tell you, I speak not from myself; but the Father who lives in me does His works. Believe me that I am in the Father, and the Father in me; or else believe me for the very works' sake. Most assuredly I tell you, He who believes in me, the works that I do, he will do also; and greater works than these will he do; because I am going to my Father. Whatever you will ask in my name, that will I do, that the Father may be glorified in the Son. If you will ask anything in my name, I will do it. If you love me, keep my commandments. I will pray to the Father, and He will give you another Counselor, that He may be with you forever,--the Spirit of truth, whom the world can't receive; for it doesn't see Him, neither knows Him. You know Him, for He lives with you, and will be in you. I will not leave you orphans. I will come to you. Yet a little while, and the world will see me no more; but you will see me. Because I live, you will live also. In that day you will know that I am in my Father, and you in me, and I in you. One who has my commandments, and keeps them, that person is one who loves me. One who loves me will be loved by my Father, and I will love him, and will reveal myself to him."*

Judas (not Iscariot, but the one also known as "Jude," or Thaddeus) said to Him, "Lord, what has happened that You are about to reveal Yourself to us, and not to the world?"

Jesus answered him, *"If a man loves me, he will keep my word. My Father will love him, and we will come to him, and make our home with him. He who doesn't love me doesn't keep my words. The word which you hear isn't mine, but the Father's who sent me. I have said these things to you, while still living with you. But the Counselor, the Holy Spirit, whom the Father will send in my name, He will teach you all things, and will remind you of all that I said to you. Peace I leave with you. My peace I give to you; not as the world gives, give I to you. Don't let your heart be troubled, neither let it be fearful. You heard how I told you, 'I go away, and I come to you.' If you loved me, you would have rejoiced, because I said 'I am going to my Father;' for the Father is greater than I. Now I have told you before it happens so that, when it happens, you may believe. I will no more speak much with you, for the prince of the world comes, and he has nothing in me. But that the world may know that I love the Father, and as the Father commanded me, even so I do. Arise, let us go from here.*

"I am the true vine, and my Father is the farmer. Every branch in me that doesn't bear fruit, He takes away. Every branch that bears fruit, He prunes, that it may bear more fruit. You are already pruned clean

because of the word which I have spoken to you. Remain in me, and I in you. As the branch can't bear fruit by itself, unless it remains in the vine, so neither can you, unless you remain in me. I am the vine. You are the branches. He who remains in me, and I in him, the same bears much fruit, for apart from me you can do nothing. If a man doesn't remain in me, he is thrown out as a branch, and is withered; and they gather them, throw them into the fire, and they are burned. If you remain in me, and my words remain in you, you will ask whatever you desire, and it will be done for you.

"In this is my Father glorified, that you bear much fruit; and so you will be my disciples. Even as the Father has loved me, I also have loved you. Remain in my love. If you keep my commandments, you will remain in my love; even as I have kept my Father's commandments, and remain in His love. I have spoken these things to you, that my joy may remain in you, and that your joy may be made full.

"This is my commandment, that you love one another, even as I have loved you. Greater love has no one than this, that someone lay down his life for his friends. You are my friends, if you do whatever I command you. No longer do I call you servants, for the servant doesn't know what his lord does. But I have called you friends, for everything that I heard from my Father, I have made known to you. You didn't choose me, but I chose you, and appointed you, that you should go and bear fruit, and that your fruit should remain; that whatever you will ask of the Father in my name, He may give it to you.

"I command these things to you, that you may love one another. If the world hates you, you know that it has hated me before it hated you. If you were of the world, the world would love its own. But because you are not of the world, since I chose you out of the world, therefore the world hates you. Remember the word that I said to you: 'A servant is not greater than his lord.' If they persecuted me, they will also persecute you. If they kept my word, they will keep yours also. But all these things will they do to you for my name's sake, because they don't know Him who sent me. If I had not come and spoken to them, they would not have had sin; but now they have no excuse for their sin. He who hates me, hates my Father also. If I hadn't done among them the

works which no one else did, they wouldn't have had sin. But now have they seen and also hated both me and my Father. But this happened so that the word may be fulfilled which was written in their law, 'They hated me without a cause.'

"When the Counselor has come, whom I will send to you from the Father, the Spirit of truth, who proceeds from the Father, He will testify about me. You will also testify, because you have been with me from the beginning.

"These things have I spoken to you, so that you wouldn't be caused to stumble. They will put you out of the synagogues. Yes, the time comes that whoever kills you will think that he offers service to God. They will do these things* because they have not known the Father, nor me. But I have told you these things, so that when the time comes, you may remember that I told you about them. I didn't tell you these things from the beginning, because I was with you. But now I am going to Him who sent me, and none of you asks me, 'Where are You going?' But because I have told you these things, sorrow has filled your heart. Nevertheless I tell you the truth: It is to your advantage that I go away, for if I don't go away, the Counselor won't come to you. But if I go, I will send Him to you. When He has come, He will convict the world about sin, about righteousness, and about judgment; about sin, because they don't believe in me; about righteousness, because I am going to my Father, and you won't see me any more; about judgment, because the prince of this world has been judged.

"I have yet many things to tell you, but you can't bear them now. However when He, the Spirit of truth, has come, He will guide you into all truth, for He will not speak from Himself; but whatever He hears, He will speak. He will declare to you things that are coming. He will glorify me, for he will take from what is mine, and will declare it to you. All things whatever the Father has are mine; therefore I said that He takes of mine, and will declare it to you. A little while, and you will not see me. Again a little while, and you will see me."

Some of His disciples therefore said to one another, "What is this that He says to us, *'A little while, and you won't see me, and again a little while, and you will see me;'* and, *'Because I go to the Father?'"* They said therefore, "What is this that He says, *'A little while?'* We don't know what He is saying."

Therefore Jesus perceived that they wanted to ask Him, and He said to them, *"Do you inquire among yourselves concerning this, that I said, 'A little while, and you won't see me, and again a little while, and you will see me?' Most assuredly I tell you, that you will weep and lament, but the world will rejoice. You will be sorrowful, but your sorrow will be turned into joy. A woman, when she gives birth, has sorrow, because her time has come. But when she has delivered the child, she doesn't remember the anguish any more, for the joy that a human being is born into the world. Therefore you now have sorrow, but I will see you again, and your heart will rejoice, and no one will take your joy away from you.*

"In that day you will ask me no questions. Most assuredly I tell you, whatever you may ask of the Father in my name, He will give it to you. Until now, you have asked nothing in my name. Ask, and you will receive, that your joy may be made full. I have spoken these things to you in figures of speech. But the time is coming when I will no more speak to you in figures of speech, but will tell you plainly about the Father. In that day you will ask in my name; and I don't say to you, that I will pray to the Father for you, for the Father Himself loves you, because you have loved me, and have believed that I came forth from God. I came out from the Father, and have come into the world. Again, I leave the world, and go to the Father."

His disciples said to Him, "Behold, now you speak plainly, and speak no figures of speech. Now we know that You know all things, and don't need for anyone to question You. By this we believe that You came forth from God."

Jesus answered them, *"Do you now believe? Behold, the time is coming, yes, and has now come, that you will be scattered, everyone to his own place, and you will leave me alone. Yet I am not alone, because the Father is with me. I have told you these things, that in me you may have peace. In the world you have oppression; but cheer up! I have overcome the world."*

Jesus said these things, and lifting up His eyes to heaven, He said, *"Father, the time has come. Glorify Your Son, that Your Son may also glorify You; even as You gave Him authority over all flesh, He will give eternal life to all whom You have given Him. This is eternal life, that they should know You, the only true God, and Him whom you sent, Jesus Christ. I glorified You on the earth. I have accomplished the work which You have given me to do. Now, Father, glorify me with Your own self with the glory which I had with you before the world existed. I revealed Your name to the people whom You have given me out of the world. They were Yours, and You have given them to me. They have kept Your word. Now they have known that all things whatever You have given me are from You, for the words which You have given me I have given to them, and they received them, and knew for sure that I came forth from You, and they have believed that You sent me. I pray for them. I don't pray for the world, but for those whom You have given me, for they are Yours. All things that are mine are Yours, and Yours are mine, and I am glorified in them. I am no more in the world, but these are in the world, and I am coming to You. Holy Father, keep them through Your name which You have given me, that they may be one, even as we are. While I was with them in the world, I kept them in Your name. Those whom You have given me I have kept. None of them is lost, except the son of destruction, that the Scripture might be fulfilled. But now I come to you, and I say these things in the world, that they may have my joy made full in themselves. I have given them Your word. The world hated them, because they are not of the world, even as I am not of the world. I pray not that you would take them from the world, but that You would keep them from the evil one. They are not of the world even as I am not of the world. Sanctify them in Your truth. Your Word is truth. As You sent me into the world, even so I have sent them into the world. For their sakes I sanctify myself, that they themselves also may be sanctified in truth. Not for these only do I pray, but for those also who believe in me through their word, that they may all be one; even as You, Father, are in me, and I in You, that they also may be one in us; that the world may believe that You sent me. The glory which You have given me, I have given to them; that they may be one, even as we are one; I in them, and You in me, that they may be perfected into one; that the world may know that You sent me, and loved them, even as You loved me. Father, I desire that they also whom You have given me be with me where I am, that they may see my glory, which You have given me, for You loved me before the foundation of the world. Righteous Father, the world hasn't known You, but I knew You; and these knew that You sent me. I made known to them Your name, and will make it known; that the love with which You loved me may be in them, and I in them."*—[John 14:1-17:26]

GETHSEMANE

Then Jesus went with His disciples to a place called Gethsemane, and He said to them, *"Sit here while I go over there and pray."* He took Peter and the two sons of Zebedee, James and John, along with Him, and He began to be sorrowful and troubled. He said to them, *"My soul is overwhelmed with sorrow to the point of death. Stay here and keep watch with me."*

Going a little farther, He knelt down and fell with His face to the ground and prayed, *"Father, if You are willing, take this cup from me; yet not my will, but Yours be done."* An angel from heaven appeared to Him and strengthened Him. And being in anguish, He prayed more earnestly, and His sweat was like drops of blood falling to the ground.

Then He returned to His disciples and found them sleeping. *"Simon,"* He said to Peter, *"are you asleep? Couldn't you keep watch for one hour? Watch and pray so that you will not fall into temptation. The spirit is willing, but the flesh is weak."*

He went away a second time and prayed, *"My Father, if it is not possible for this cup to be taken away unless I drink it, may Your will be done."* When He came back, He again found them sleeping, because their eyes were heavy. They did not know what to say to Him.

So He left them and went away once more and prayed the third time, saying the same thing. Then He returned to the disciples and said to them,

"Are you still sleeping and resting? Look, the hour has come, and the Son of Man is delivered into the hands of sinners. Rise! Let us go! Here comes my betrayer!"—[Matthew 26:36-46, Mark 14:32-42, Luke 22:39-46]

CHAPTER 21

JESUS' ARREST

While Jesus was still speaking, Judas, one of the Twelve, arrived. With him was a large crowd armed with swords and clubs, sent from the chief priests, the teachers of the law, and the elders of the people. Judas was leading them. Jesus, knowing all that was going to happen to Him, went out and asked them, *"Who is it you want?"*

"Jesus of Nazareth," they replied.

"I am He," Jesus said. (And Judas the traitor was standing there with them.) When Jesus said, *"I am He,"* they drew back and fell to the ground. Again He asked them, *"Who is it you want?"*

"Jesus of Nazareth," they said.

Jesus answered, *"I told you that I am He. If you are looking for me, then let these men go."* This happened so that the words He had spoken would be fulfilled: "I have not lost one of those You gave me."

Now the betrayer had arranged a signal with them (to ensure the right man was apprehended): "The one I kiss is the man; arrest Him and lead Him away under guard." Going at once to Jesus, Judas said, "Greetings, Rabbi!" and kissed Him.

Jesus replied, *"Do what you came for, friend."* Then the men stepped forward, seized Jesus and arrested Him.

When Jesus' followers saw what was going to happen, they said, "Lord, should we strike with our swords?" And one of Jesus' companions, Simon Peter, reached for his sword, drew it out and struck the servant of the high priest, cutting off his right ear. The servant's name was Malchus.

But Jesus answered, *"No more of this!"* And He touched Malchus' ear and healed him. *"Put your sword back in its place,"* Jesus said to him, *"for all who draw the sword will die by the sword. Do you think I cannot call on my Father, and He will at once put at my disposal more than twelve legions of angels? But how then would the Scriptures be fulfilled that say it must happen in this way?"*

In that hour Jesus said to the crowd, *"Am I leading a rebellion, or am I a robber, that you have come out with swords and clubs to capture me? Every day I sat in the temple courts teaching, and you did not lay a hand on me. But all this has happened so that the Scriptures of the prophets would be fulfilled. This is your hour—when darkness reigns."*

Then all the disciples deserted Him and fled. A young man, wearing nothing but a linen garment, was following Jesus. When they seized him, he escaped and fled naked, leaving his garment behind.—[Matthew 26:47-56, Mark 14:43-52, Luke 22:47-53, John 18:1-11]

JESUS and the SANHEDRIN

So the detachment, the commanding officer, and the officers of the Jews, who had seized Jesus bound Him, and led Him to Annas first, for he was father-in-law to Caiaphas, who was high priest that year. Now it was Caiaphas who advised the Jews that it was expedient that one man should perish for the people. Simon Peter followed Jesus from a distance, as did another disciple. Now that disciple was known to the high priest, and entered in with Jesus into the court of the high priest; but Peter was standing at the door outside. So the other disciple, who was known to the high priest, went out and spoke to her who kept the door, and brought in Peter. The maid asked Peter, "You also were with Jesus the Galilean. Are you also not one of this man's disciples?" He said, "I am not." Now the servants and the officers were standing there, having made a fire of coals, for it was cold. They were warming themselves. Peter joined them, initially standing and warming himself. After some time, they sat down, and Peter sitting with them continued to warm himself in the light of the fire.

Meanwhile, the high priest questioned Jesus about His disciples and His teaching. "I have spoken openly to the world," Jesus replied. *"I always taught in synagogues or at the temple, where all the Jews come together. I said nothing in secret. Why question me? Ask those who heard me. Surely they know what I said."* When Jesus said this, one of the officials nearby slapped Him in the face. "Is this the way you answer the high priest?" he demanded. *"If I said something wrong,"* Jesus replied, *"testify as to what is wrong. But if I spoke the truth, why did you strike me?"* —[John 18:12-14, 18:15-18, 18:19-24]

PETER DENIES JESUS

Meanwhile, as Peter was in the courtyard below, one of the other maids of the high priest came. She had seen Peter standing and warming himself. Having studied him closely as he sat by the light, she said to some of the bystanders "That man was also with Jesus, the Nazarene!" Hearing this, they said, "You aren't also one of his disciples, are you?"

But he denied it before them all, saying, "I don't know what you are talking about."

When he had gone out onto the porch, someone else saw him, and said to those who were there, "You're definitely one of them, for your accent betrays you!

Then he began to curse and to swear, "I don't know what you're talking about! I said, 'I don't know the man!'"

Immediately the rooster crowed. And the Lord turned and looked at Peter. And Peter remembered the word which Jesus had said to him, "Before the rooster crows today, you will disown me three times." And he went outside and wept bitterly. —[Matthew 26:69-75, Mark 14:66-72, Luke 22:55-62]

JESUS BEFORE CAIAPHAS

Annas sent Him bound to Caiaphas, the high priest. At daybreak, the council of the elders of the people, both the chief priests and the teachers of the law, met together, and Jesus was led before them. The chief priests, the elders, and the whole council sought false testimony against Jesus, that they might put Him to death; and they found none. For even though many gave false testimony against Him, their testimony didn't agree with each other.

At last two false witnesses came forward, and said, "This man said, 'I am able to destroy the temple of God that is made with human hands, and to rebuild it in three days without hands.'" Even so, their testimony did not agree.

The high priest stood up in the midst, and asked Jesus, "Have You no answer? What is it which these testify against You?" But He stayed quiet, and answered nothing. The high priest asked Him, "Are You the Christ, the Son of the Blessed?" But Jesus held His peace. The high priest answered Him, "I adjure You by the living God, that You tell us whether You are the Christ, the Son of God!"

Jesus answered, *"If I tell you, you will not believe me, and if I asked you, you would not answer. I tell you, you will see the Son of Man sitting at the right hand of the mighty God; that is at the right hand of Power, and coming with the clouds of the sky."*

They all asked, "Are you then the Son of God?"

He replied, *"You say that I AM.*

The high priest tore his clothes, and said, "What further need have we of witnesses and testimony? You have heard the blasphemy! We have heard it from His own lips! What do you think?" They all answered condemningly, "He is worthy of death!" Some began to spit on Him, and to cover His face, and to beat Him with fists, while others slapped Him, and they said, "Prophesy to us, You Christ! Who hit You?" —[Matthew 26:57-68, Mark 14:53-65, Luke 22:66-71, John 18:24]

JESUS STANDS BEFORE PILATE

Early in the morning, all the chief priests and the elders of the people made their plans on how to have Jesus executed. They bound Him. Then the whole assembly rose and led Him from Caiaphas over to Pilate, the Roman governor.

Since it was early morning, to avoid ceremonial uncleanness, they did not enter the palace; because they wanted to be able to eat the Passover. So Pilate came out to them and asked, "What charges are you bringing against this man?"

"If He were not a criminal," they replied, "we would not have handed Him over to you."

Pilate said, "Take Him yourselves and judge Him by your own law."

"But we have no right to execute anyone," they objected. This took place to fulfill what Jesus had said about the kind of death He was going to die.—[Matthew 27:1-2; Mark 15:1; Luke 22:66-23:4, and John 18:28-32]

JUDAS HANGS HIMSELF

Then Judas, who betrayed Him, when he saw that Jesus was condemned, felt remorse, and brought back the thirty pieces of silver to the chief priests and elders, saying, "I have sinned in that I betrayed innocent blood."

But they said, "What is that to us? You see to it."

He threw down the pieces of silver in the sanctuary, and departed. He went away and hanged himself. The chief priests took the pieces of silver, and said, "It's not lawful to put them into the treasury, since it is the price of blood." They took counsel, and bought the potter's field with them, to bury strangers in. Therefore that field was called "The Field of Blood" to this day. Then that which was spoken through Jeremiah the prophet was fulfilled, saying,

"They took the thirty pieces of silver,

The price of Him upon whom a price had been set,

Whom some of the children of Israel priced,

And they gave them for the potter's field,

As the Lord commanded me."—[Matthew 27:3-10]

Meanwhile, Pilate, who had once more entered the palace, summoned Jesus. When Jesus stood before the governor, the governor asked him, "Are You the king of the Jews?"

"Is that your own idea," Jesus asked, *"or did others talk to you about me?"*

"Am I a Jew?" Pilate replied. "Your own people and chief priests handed You over to me. What is it You have done?"

Jesus said, *"My kingdom is not of this world. If it were, my servants would fight to prevent my arrest by the Jewish leaders. But now my kingdom is from another place."*

"You are a king, then!" said Pilate.

Jesus answered, *"You say that I am a king. In fact, the reason I was born and came into the world is to testify to the truth. Everyone on the side of truth listens to me."*

"What is truth?" retorted Pilate. With this, he went out again to the Jews gathered there and said, "I find no basis for a charge against Him."

But they insisted, "He stirs up the people all over Judea by His teaching. He started in Galilee and has come all the way here."

When Pilate heard this, he asked if the man was a Galilean. On hearing that Jesus was under Herod's jurisdiction, he sent Him to Herod Antipas, who was also in Jerusalem at that time. —[Matthew 27:11-14, Mark 15:2-5, Luke 23:2-7, and John 18:33-38 *harmonized*]

JESUS BEFORE HEROD

Now when Herod saw Jesus, he was exceedingly glad, for he had wanted to see Him for a long time, because he had heard many things about Him. He hoped to see some miracle done by Him. He questioned Him with many words, but Jesus gave no answers. The chief priests and the scribes stood, vehemently accusing Him. Herod with his soldiers humiliated Jesus and mocked Him. Dressing Him in luxurious clothing, they sent him back to Pilate. Herod and Pilate became friends with each other that very day, for before that they were enemies with each other.—[Luke 23:6-12]

Pilate called together the chief priests and the rulers and the people, and said to them, "You brought this man to me as one that perverts the people, and see, I have examined Him before you, and found no basis for a charge against this man concerning those things of which you accuse Him. Neither has Herod, for he sent Him back to us, and see, nothing worthy of death has been done by Him. I will therefore chastise Him and release Him." —[Luke 23:6-16]

CHAPTER 22

JESUS SENTENCED TO DEATH & BARABBAS FREED

Now it was the governor's custom at the festival to release a prisoner chosen by the crowd. A man called Barabbas was in prison with the insurrectionists who had committed murder in an uprising. The crowd came up and asked Pilate to do for them what he usually did.—[Matthew 27:15-17; Mark 15:6-8; Luke 23:18-19; John 18:39-40]

"Do you want me to release to you the king of the Jews?" asked Pilate, knowing it was out of self-interest that the chief priests had handed Jesus over to him.—[Matthew 27:18 and Mark 15:9-10]

While Pilate was sitting on the judge's seat, his wife sent him this message: "Don't have anything to do with that innocent man, for I have suffered a great deal today in a dream because of Him."—[Matthew 27:19]

But the chief priests and the elders persuaded the crowd to ask for Barabbas and to have Jesus executed. "Which of the two do you want me to release to you?" asked the governor.—[Matthew 27:20-21; Mark 15:11]

"Barabbas," they answered.—[Matthew 27:21; Mark 15:11]

"What shall I do, then, with Jesus who is called the Messiah?" Pilate asked (Matthew 27:22; Mark 15:12).

They all answered, "Crucify Him!" (Matthew 27:22-23; Mark 15:13-14).

"Why? What crime has He committed?" asked Pilate (Matthew 27:23; Mark 15:14).

But they shouted all the louder, "Crucify Him!" (Matthew 27:23; Mark 15:14).

When He was accused by the chief priests and the elders, He gave no answer. Then Pilate asked Him, "Don't You hear the testimony they are bringing against You?" But Jesus made no reply, not even to a single charge—to the great amazement of the governor (Matthew 27:12-14; Mark 15:4-5).

The chief priests accused Him of many things. So again Pilate asked Him, "Aren't You going to answer? See how many things they are accusing You of." But Jesus still made no reply, and Pilate was amazed (Mark 15:3-5).

Pilate decreed that what they asked for should be done. He released him who had been thrown into prison for insurrection and murder, for whom they asked, but he delivered Jesus up to their will (Luke 23:24-25).

Then Pilate took Jesus and had Him flogged (Matthew 27:26; Mark 15:15; John 19:1).

The governor's soldiers took Jesus into the Praetorium and gathered the whole company of soldiers around Him. They stripped Him and put a scarlet robe on Him, twisted together a crown of thorns, and set it on His head. They put a staff in His right hand. Then they knelt in front of Him and mocked Him. "Hail, king of the Jews!" they said. They spit on Him, and took the staff and struck Him on the head again and again. They struck Him in the face (Matthew 27:27-30; Mark 15:16-19; John 19:2-3).

Once more Pilate came out and said to the Jews gathered there, "Look, I am bringing Him out to you to let you know that I find no basis for a charge against Him." When Jesus came out wearing the crown of thorns and the purple robe, Pilate said to them, "Here is the man!" (John 19:4-5).

As soon as the chief priests and their officials saw Him, they shouted, "Crucify! Crucify!" But Pilate answered, "You take Him and crucify Him. As for me, I find no basis for a charge against Him" (John 19:6).

The Jewish leaders insisted, "We have a law, and according to that law He must die, because He claimed to be the Son of God" (John 19:7).

Now he had to release one prisoner to them at the feast. But they all cried out together, saying, "Away with this man! Release to us Barabbas!" (Luke 23:17-19).

Then Pilate spoke to them again, wanting to release Jesus, but they shouted, saying, "Crucify! Crucify Him!" (Luke 23:20-21).

He said to them the third time, "Why? What evil has this man done? I have found no capital crime in Him. I will therefore chastise Him and release Him." But they were urgent with loud voices, asking that He might be crucified. Their voices and the voices of the chief priests prevailed (Luke 23:22-23).

When Pilate heard this, he was even more afraid, and he went back inside the palace. "Where do You come from?" he asked Jesus, but Jesus gave him no answer. "Do You refuse to speak to me?" Pilate said. "Don't You realize I have power either to free You or to crucify You?" (John 19:8-10).

Jesus answered, "You would have no power over me if it were not given to you from above. Therefore the one who handed me over to you is guilty of a greater sin" (John 19:11).

From then on, Pilate tried to set Jesus free, but the Jewish leaders kept shouting, "If you let this man go, you are no friend of Caesar. Anyone who claims to be a king opposes Caesar" (John 19:12).

When Pilate heard this, he brought Jesus out and sat down on the judge's seat at a place known as the Stone Pavement (which in Aramaic is Gabbatha). It was the day of Preparation of the Passover; it was about noon (John 19:13-14).

"Here is your king," Pilate said to the Jews (John 19:14).

But they shouted, "Take Him away! Take Him away! Crucify Him!" (John 19:15).

"Shall I crucify your king?" Pilate asked (John 19:15).

"We have no king but Caesar," the chief priests answered (John 19:15).

Finally, Pilate handed Him over to them to be crucified. When they had mocked Him, they took off the robe and put His own clothes on Him. Then they led Him away to crucify Him (Matthew 27:31; Mark 15:20; John 19:16).

VIA DOLOROSA (THE WAY OF SUFFERING)

As they were going out, they met a man from Cyrene, named Simon, the father of Alexander and Rufus. He was passing by on his way in from the country, and they forced him to carry the cross. They seized Simon and as they led Jesus away, they put the cross on him and made him carry it behind the Christ (Matthew 27:32; Mark 15:21; Luke 23:26).

A great multitude of the people followed him, including women who also mourned and lamented him. But Jesus, turning to them, said, "Daughters of Jerusalem, don't weep for me, but weep for yourselves and for your children. For behold, the days are coming in which they will say, 'Blessed are the barren, childless women, the wombs that never bore, and the breasts that never nursed.' Then they will begin to say to the mountains, 'Fall on us!' and to the hills, 'Cover us.' For if they do these things in the green tree, what will be done in the dry?" (Luke 23:27-31).

Two other men, both criminals, were also led out with Him to be executed (Luke 23:32).

Carrying His own cross, He went out to the place of the Skull (which in Aramaic is called Golgotha). There they crucified Him, along with the criminals, one on the right and the other on the left (Luke 23:33; Matthew 27:38; Mark 15:27).

Pilate had a notice prepared and fastened to the cross. It read: "JESUS OF NAZARETH, THE KING OF THE JEWS." The sign was written in Aramaic, Latin, and Greek. The chief priests of the Jews protested to Pilate, "Do not write 'The King of the Jews,' but that this man claimed to be king of the Jews." Pilate answered, "What I have written, I have written."

Jesus said, *"Father, forgive them, for they don't know what they are doing."*

When the soldiers crucified Jesus, they took His clothes, dividing them into four shares, one for each of them, with the undergarment remaining. This garment was seamless, woven in one piece from top to bottom. "Let's not tear it," they said to one another. "Let's decide by lot who will get it." This happened that the scripture might be fulfilled that said, "They divided my clothes among them and cast lots for my garment." So this is what the soldiers did.

(Luke 23:34; Matthew 27:35; Mark 15:24; John 19:23-24).

The people stood watching. The rulers with them also scoffed at Him, saying, "He saved others. Let Him save Himself, if this is the Christ of God, His chosen one!" (Luke 23:35).

The soldiers also mocked Him, coming to Him and offering Him vinegar, and saying, "If You are the King of the Jews, save Yourself!" (Luke 23:36-37; Matthew 27:39-44; Mark 15:29-32; John 19:29).

THE CRUCIFIXION

And sitting down, they kept watch over Him there. Those who passed by hurled insults at Him, shaking their heads and saying, "So! You who are going to destroy the temple and build it in three days, save Yourself! Come down from the cross, if You are the Son of God!" In the same way, the chief priests, the teachers of the law, and the elders mocked Him. "He saved others," they said, "but He can't save Himself! He's the king of Israel! Let Him come down now from the cross, and we will believe in Him. He trusts in God. Let God rescue Him now if He wants Him, for He said, 'I am the Son of God.'" In the same way, the rebels who were crucified with Him also heaped insults on Him.

One of the criminals who hung there hurled insults at Him: "Aren't You the Messiah? Save Yourself and us!" But the other criminal rebuked Him. "Don't you fear God," he said, "since you are under the same sentence? We are punished justly, for we are getting what our deeds deserve. But this man has done nothing wrong." Then he said, "Jesus, remember me when You come into Your kingdom."

Jesus answered Him, *"Truly I tell you, today you will be with me in paradise."*

Near the cross of Jesus stood His mother, His mother's sister, Mary the wife of Clopas, and Mary Magdalene. When Jesus saw His mother there, and the disciple whom He loved standing nearby, He said to her, *"Woman, here is your son,"* and to the disciple, *"Here is your mother."* From that time on, this disciple took her into his home.—[Matthew 27:33-44, Mark 15:22-32, Luke 23:33-43, John 19:17-27]

JESUS' DEATH

From noon until three in the afternoon, darkness came over all the land. About three in the afternoon, the sun was darkened. Jesus cried out in a loud voice, *"Eli, Eli, lema sabachthani?"* (which means *"My God, my God, why have You forsaken me?"*).

When some of those standing there heard this, they said, "He's calling Elijah." Later, knowing that everything had now been finished, and so that Scripture would be fulfilled, Jesus said, *"I am thirsty."* A jar of wine vinegar was there, so they soaked a sponge in it, put the sponge on a stalk of the hyssop plant, and lifted it to Jesus' lips. When He had received the drink, Jesus said, *"It is finished."*

At that moment, the curtain of the temple was torn in two from top to bottom. And when Jesus had cried out with a loud voice, He said, **"Father, 'into Your hands I commit My spirit."** Having said this, He breathed His last and bowing His head, gave up His Spirit.

The earth shook, the rocks split, and the tombs broke open. When the centurion and those with him who were guarding Jesus saw the earthquake and all that had happened, they were terrified and exclaimed, "Surely He was the Son of God!" The centurion, seeing what had happened, praised God and said, "Surely this was a righteous man!"

Some women were watching from a distance. Among them were Mary Magdalene, Mary the mother of James the younger and of Joseph, and Salome. In Galilee these women had followed Him and cared for His needs. Many other women who had come up with Him to Jerusalem were also there.

All the people who had gathered to witness this sight saw what took place, they beat their breasts and went away. But all those who knew Him, including the women who had followed Him from Galilee, stood at a distance, watching these things.—[Matthew 27:45-56, Mark 15:33-41, Luke 23:44-49, John 19:28-30]

Therefore the Jews, because it was the Preparation Day, so that the bodies wouldn't remain on the cross on the Sabbath (for that Sabbath was a special one), asked of Pilate that their legs might be broken, and that they might be taken away. Therefore the soldiers came, and broke the legs of the first, and of the other who was crucified with Him; but when they came to Jesus, and saw that He was already dead, they didn't break His legs. However one of the soldiers pierced His side with a spear, and immediately blood and water came out. He who has seen has testified, and his testimony is true. He knows that he tells the truth, that you may believe. For these things happened, that the Scripture might be fulfilled, "A bone of Him will not be broken." Again another Scripture says, "They will look on Him whom they pierced."—[John 19:31-37]

As evening approached, there came a rich man from Arimathea, named Joseph, who had himself become a disciple of Jesus. Now Joseph was a member of the Council, a good and upright man, who had not consented to their decision and action. He was waiting for the kingdom of God.

Going to Pilate, he asked him for Jesus' body; doing so secretly because he feared the Jews. Pilate was surprised to hear that he was already dead. Summoning the centurion, he asked him if Jesus had already died. When he learned from the centurion that it was so, he permitted Joseph to take the corpse.

Joseph took the body down, wrapped it in a clean linen cloth, and placed it in his own new tomb that he had cut out of the rock, in which no one had ever been laid. He rolled a big stone in front of the entrance to the tomb and went away.

He was accompanied by Nicodemus, the man who much earlier had visited Jesus at night. Nicodemus brought a mixture of myrrh and aloes, about seventy-five pounds. Taking Jesus' body, the two of them wrapped it, with the spices, in strips of linen. This was in accordance with Jewish burial customs.

Now at the place where He was crucified, was a garden, and in the garden, a new tomb in which no one had yet been laid. They laid Jesus there because the Jewish day of Preparation was at hand and this tomb was nearby. The women who had come with Jesus from Galilee followed Joseph and saw the tomb and how His body was laid in it. Mary Magdalene and Mary the mother of Joseph saw where He was laid. Then they went home and prepared spices and perfumes. But they rested on the Sabbath in obedience to the commandment.—[Matthew 27:57-61, Mark 15:42-47, Luke 23:50-56, John 19:38-42]

GUARDING THE TOMB

Now on the next day, which was the day after the Preparation Day, the chief priests and the Pharisees were gathered together to Pilate, saying, "Sir, we remember what that deceiver said while He was still alive: 'After three days I will rise again.' Command therefore that the tomb be made secure until the third day, lest perhaps His disciples come at night and steal Him away, and tell the people, 'He is risen from the dead;' and the last deception will be worse than the first."

Pilate said to them, "You have a guard. Go, make it as secure as you can." So they went with the guard and made the tomb secure, sealing the stone.—[Matthew 27:62-66]

CHAPTER 23

THE RESURRECTION THE EARTHQUAKE and THE ANGELS

Now after the Sabbath, as it began to dawn on the first day of the week, Mary Magdalene and the other Mary came to look at the grave. And behold, a severe earthquake had occurred, for an angel of the Lord descended from heaven, rolled away the stone, and sat upon it. His appearance was like lightning, and his clothing as white as snow. The guards shook for fear of him and became like dead men.—[Matthew 28:1-4]

Now on this day, Mary Magdalene had come first to the tomb, having set out while it was still dark, and when she arrived, she saw the stone already removed from the entrance of the tomb. So she ran to Simon Peter and to the other disciple whom Jesus loved, and said to them, "They have removed the Lord from the tomb, and we do not know where they have laid Him."—[John 20:1-2]

So Peter and the other disciple went forth, and headed to the tomb. The two ran together; and the other disciple ran ahead faster than Peter and came to the tomb first, and stooping and looking in, he saw the linen wrappings lying there. While he hesitated to enter, Simon Peter, having caught up to him, entered the tomb; and he saw the linen wrappings lying there, and the face-cloth which had been on His head, not lying with the linen wrappings, but rolled up in a place by itself. So the other disciple who had first come to the tomb then also entered, and he saw and believed (in the resurrection of Christ). For as yet they did not understand the Scripture, that He must rise again from the dead. So the disciples went away again to their own homes. Peter marveled at what had happened.—[John 20:3-10, Luke 24:13]

MARY MAGDALENE'S ENCOUNTER with THE RISEN LORD

But Mary stood outside the tomb weeping; and as she wept, she stooped and looked into the tomb; and suddenly saw two angels clothed in white sitting, one at the head and one at the feet, where the body of Jesus had been lying. And they said to her, "Woman, why are you weeping?" She said to them, "Because they have taken away my Lord, and I do not know where they have laid Him." When she had said this, she turned around and saw Jesus standing there, and did not know that it was Him. Jesus said to her, "Woman, why are you weeping? Whom are you seeking?" Supposing Him to be the gardener, she said to Him, "Sir, if you have carried Him away, tell me where you have laid Him, and I will take Him away." Jesus said to her, "Mary!" She turned and said to Him in Hebrew, "Rabboni!" (which means,

Teacher). Jesus said to her, "Stop clinging to me, for I have not yet ascended to the Father; but go to my brethren and say to them, *'I ascend to my Father and your Father, and my God and your God.'"* Thus, Jesus appeared first to Mary Magdalene, from whom He had cast out seven demons. Mary Magdalene, coming to the disciples as they mourned and wept, announced the good news, saying, "I have seen Him," and also all that He had said to her. When they heard that He was alive, and had been seen by her, they disbelieved.—[John 20:11-18, and Mark 16:9-11]

THE OTHER WOMEN VISIT THE TOMB

After Mary Magdalene had visited the tomb, Mary (the wife of Cleopa, and also the mother of James and Joses), along with Salome, Joanna, and the other women bought spices, so that they might come and anoint Him. Very early on the first day of the week, they came to the tomb when the sun had risen. They were saying to one another, "Who will roll away the stone for us from the entrance of the tomb?" Looking up, they saw that the stone had been rolled away, although it was extremely large. When they entered the tomb, they did not find the body of the Lord Jesus. While they were perplexed about this, behold, two men suddenly stood near them in dazzling clothing; and as the women were terrified and bowed their faces to the ground, the men said to them, "Why do you seek the living One among the dead? He is not here, but He has risen. Remember how He spoke to you while He was still in Galilee, saying that the Son of Man must be delivered into the hands of sinful men, and be crucified, and the third day rise again." And they remembered His words... —[Mark 16:1-4; Luke 24:1-8]

And behold, Jesus met them along the way and greeted them. And they came up and took hold of His feet and worshiped His. Then Hie said to them, "Do not be afraid; go and take word to my brethren to leave for Galilee, and there they will see me."—[Matthew 28:9-10]

THE GUARD'S REPORT

Now while the women were going to the apostles, behold, some of the guards came into the city, and told the chief priests all the things that had happened. When they were assembled with the elders, and had taken counsel, they gave a large amount of silver to the soldiers, saying, "Say that His disciples came by night, and stole Him away while we slept. If this comes to the governor's ears, we will persuade him and make you free of worry." So they took the money and did as they were told. This saying was spread abroad among the Jews, and continues until this day.—[Matthew 28:11-15]

Even so, the truth cannot be hidden, for not only had Jesus resurrected from the grave to be seen by the eyes of multiple witnesses, but the bodies of many holy people who had died had also been raised to life. They came out of the tombs after Jesus' resurrection and went into the holy city appearing to many people.—[Matthew 27:52-53]

THE DISCIPLES HEAR THE NEWS

The women returned from the tomb, and reported all these things to the eleven and to all the rest. Now they who were sharing the news of His resurrection with the apostles were Mary Magdalene, Joanna, Mary the mother of James; and also the other women with them. But these words appeared to them as nonsense, and they would not believe them.—[Luke 24:9-11]

THE ROAD TO EMMAUS

After these things, Jesus was revealed in another form. And behold, two of them were going into the country that very day to a village named Emmaus, which was about seven miles from Jerusalem. And they were talking with each other about all these things which had taken place. While they were talking and discussing, Jesus Himself approached and began traveling with them. But their eyes were prevented from recognizing Him. And He said to them, "What are these words that you are exchanging with

one another as you are walking?" And they stood still, looking sad. One of
them, named Cleopas, answered and said to Him, "Are You the only one
visiting Jerusalem and unaware of the things which have happened here in
these days?" And He said to them, "What things?" And they said to Him,
"The things about Jesus the Nazarene, who was a prophet mighty in deed
and word in the sight of God and all the people, and how the chief priests
and our rulers delivered Him to the sentence of death, and crucified Him.
But we were hoping that it was He who was going to redeem Israel. Indeed,
besides all this, it is the third day since these things happened. But also
some women among us amazed us. When they were at the tomb early in
the morning, and did not find His body, they came, saying that they had
also seen a vision of angels, who said that He was alive. Some of those who
were with us went to the tomb and found it just exactly as the women also
had said; but Him they did not see." And He said to them, "O foolish men
and slow of heart to believe in all that the prophets have spoken! Was it not
necessary for the Christ to suffer these things and to enter into His glory?"
Then beginning with Moses and with all the prophets, He explained to
them the things concerning Himself in all the Scriptures. And they
approached the village where they were going, and He acted as though He
were going farther. But they urged Him, saying, "Stay with us, for it is
getting toward evening, and the day is now nearly over." So He went in to
stay with them. When He had reclined at the table with them, He took the
bread and blessed it, and breaking it, He began giving it to them. Then their
eyes were opened and they recognized Him; and He vanished from their
sight. They said to one another, "Were not our hearts burning within us
while He was speaking to us on the road, while He was explaining the
Scriptures to us?" And they got up that very hour, went away, returning to
Jerusalem, and found gathered together, the eleven and those who were
with them, saying, "The Lord has really risen and has appeared to Simon."
They began to relate their experiences on the road and how He was
recognized by them in the breaking of the bread. The apostles didn't
believe them either —[Luke 24:13-35 and Mark 16:12-13]

JESUS APPEARS TO THE DISCIPLES

While they were telling these things, He Himself stood in their midst and said to them, "Peace be to you." But they were startled and frightened and thought that they were seeing a spirit. And He said to them, "Why are you troubled, and why do doubts arise in your hearts? See my hands and my feet, that it is I myself; touch me and see, for a spirit does not have flesh and bones as you see that I have." And when He had said this, He reprimanded them for their unbelief and hardness of heart, because they had not believed those who had seen Him after He had risen from the dead. He showed them His hands, His feet, and His side. The disciples therefore were glad when they saw the Lord. Jesus therefore said to them again, "Peace be to you. As the Father has sent me, even so I send you." When He had said this, He breathed on them, and said to them, "Receive the Holy Spirit!" Whoever's sins you forgive, they are forgiven them. Whoever's sins you retain, they have been retained. While they still could not believe it because of their joy and amazement, He said to them, "Have you anything here to eat?" They gave Him a piece of a broiled fish; and He took it and ate it before them. Now Thomas, one of the twelve, called Didymus, was not with them when Jesus came. So the other disciples were saying to him, "We have seen the Lord!" But he said to them, "Unless I see in His hands the imprint of the nails, and put my finger into the place of the nails, and put my hand into His side, I will not believe."—[Luke 24:36-43; John 20:19-25, Mark 16:14b]

JESUS APPEARS TO THOMAS

After eight days His disciples were again inside, and Thomas with them. As they were reclining at the table, Jesus came, the doors having been shut, and stood in their midst and said, "Peace be with you." Then He said to Thomas, "Reach here with your finger, and see my hands; and reach here your hand and put it into my side; and do not be unbelieving, but believing." Thomas answered and said to Him, "My Lord and my God!" Jesus said to him, "Because you have seen me, have you believed? Blessed are they who did not see, and yet believed."—[John 20:26-30, Mark 16:14a]

[30] Therefore Jesus did many other signs in the presence of his disciples, which are not written in this book; [31] but these are written that you may believe that Jesus is the Christ, the Son of God, and that believing you may have life in his name.—[John 20:31]

JESUS APPEARS BY THE SEA OF GALILEE

After these things Jesus manifested Himself again to the disciples at the Sea of Tiberias (a.k.a Sea of Galilee, Lake of Tiberius, or Kinneret) and He manifested Himself in this way. Simon Peter, and Thomas called Didymus, and Nathanael of Cana in Galilee, and the sons of Zebedee, and two others of His disciples were together. Simon Peter said to them, "I am going fishing." They said to him, "We will also come with you." They went out and got into the boat; and that night they caught nothing. Early in the morning, Jesus stood on the shore, but the disciples did not realize that it was Him. He called out to them, "Friends, haven't you any fish?" "No," they answered. He said, "Throw your net on the right side of the boat and you will find some." When they did, they were unable to haul the net in because of the large number of fish. Then the disciple whom Jesus loved said to Peter, "It is the Lord!" As soon as Simon Peter heard him say, "It is the Lord," he wrapped his outer garment around him (for he had taken it off) and jumped into the water. The other disciples followed in the boat, towing the net full of fish, for they were not far from shore, about a hundred yards. When they landed, they saw a fire of burning coals there with fish on it, and some bread. Jesus said to them, "Bring some of the fish you have just caught." So Simon Peter climbed back into the boat and dragged the net ashore. It was full of large fish, 153, but even with so many the net was not torn. Jesus said to them, "Come and have breakfast." None of the disciples dared ask Him, "Who are you?" They knew it was the Lord. Jesus came, took the bread and gave it to them, and did the same with the fish. This was now the third time He appeared to His disciples after He was raised from the dead. When they had finished eating, Jesus said to Simon Peter, "Simon son of John, do you love me more than these?" "Yes, Lord," he said, "you know that I love You." Jesus said, "Feed My lambs." Again Jesus said, "Simon son of John, do you love me?" He answered, "Yes, Lord, you know that I love You." Jesus said, "Take care of my sheep." The third time He said to him, "Simon son of John, do you love me?" Peter was hurt because Jesus asked him the third time, "Do you love me?" He said, "Lord, you know all things; you know that I love You." Jesus said, "Feed my sheep. Very truly I tell you, when you were younger you dressed yourself and went where you wanted; but when you are old you will stretch out your hands, and someone else will dress you and lead you where you do not want to go." Jesus said this to indicate the kind of death by which Peter would glorify God. Then He said to him, "Follow me!" Peter turned and saw that the disciple whom Jesus loved was following them. This was the one who had leaned back against Jesus at the supper and had said, "Lord, who is going to betray You?" When Peter saw him, he asked, "Lord, what about him?" Jesus answered, "If I want him to remain alive until I return, what is that to you? You must follow me." Because of this, the rumor spread among the believers that this disciple would not die. But Jesus did not say that he would not die; He only said, "If *I desire that he stay until I come, what is that to you?"* This is the disciple who testifies about these things, and wrote these things. We know that his witness is true. There are also many other things which Jesus did, which if they would all be written, I suppose that even the world itself wouldn't have room for the books that would be written—[John 21:1-25]

THE GREAT COMMISSION

Then the eleven disciples went to Galilee, to the mountain where Jesus had told them to go. When they saw Him, they worshiped Him; but some doubted. Then Jesus came to them and said, "All authority in heaven and on earth has been given to me. Therefore go and make disciples of all nations, baptizing them in the name of the Father and of the Son and of the Holy Spirit, and teaching them to obey everything I have commanded you. He also said to them, "Go into all the world and preach the gospel to all creation. Whoever believes and is baptized will be saved, but whoever does not believe will be condemned. And these signs will accompany those who believe: In my name they will drive out demons; they will speak in new tongues; they will pick up snakes with their hands; and when they drink deadly poison, it will not hurt them at all; they will place their hands on sick people, and they will get well." And surely I am with you always, to the very end of the age."—[Matthew 28:16-20 and Mark 16:15-18]

[44] He said to them, "This is what I told you while I was still with you, that all things which are written in the law of Moses, the prophets, and the psalms concerning me must be fulfilled."

[45] Then he opened their minds, that they might understand the Scriptures. [46] He said to them, "Thus it is written, and thus it was necessary for the Christ to suffer and to rise from the dead the third day, [47] and that repentance and remission of sins should be preached in his name to all the nations, beginning at Jerusalem. [48] You are witnesses of these things.[49] Behold, I send out the promise of my Father on you. But wait in the city of Jerusalem until you are clothed with power from on high."—[Luke 24:44-49]

THE ASCENSION OF JESUS

When He had led them out to the vicinity of Bethany, He lifted up His hands and blessed them. While He was blessing them, He left them and was taken up into heaven where He took His place and sat at the right hand of God. Then they worshiped Him and returned to Jerusalem with great joy. They stayed continually at the temple, praising God.

Then the disciples went out, preached everywhere, and the Lord worked with them and confirmed His word by the signs that accompanied it.—[Mark 16:19-20 and Luke 24:50-53]

A Message from the compiler:

Dear reader, I sincerely hope you were blessed in reading this and have an even deeper understanding of the Gospel. It was quite the adventure for me as well and I believe this can have a positive and significant impact on our faith. In fact, I pray earnestly for this. If you enjoyed the harmony presented in this book, please support by spreading the word.

Thank you and may our Lord bless you exceedingly above what you had hoped for and imagined in Jesus' precious and mighty name.

Amen!

www.ingramcontent.com/pod-product-compliance
Lightning Source LLC
Chambersburg PA
CBHW070120100426
42744CB00010B/1879